THE
KAMA SU
OF WORK

WHY WORK IS THE NEW SEX AND HOW
TO MAKE SURE YOU'RE GETTING ENOUGH

AVRIL MILLAR

THE
KAMA SUTRA
OF WORK

WHY WORK IS THE NEW SEX AND HOW TO MAKE SURE YOU'RE GETTING ENOUGH

By

Avril Millar

ISBN: 978-0-9568977-2-5

This book is published by Avril Millar in conjunction with WRITERSWORLD, and is produced entirely in the UK. It is available to order from most bookshops in the United Kingdom, and is also globally available via UK based Internet book retailers.

Edited by Esther Harris
Copy edited by Ian Large
Book cover design and visual PDFs by Tappin Gofton

WRITERSWORLD
2 Bear Close Flats, Bear Close, Woodstock
Oxfordshire, OX20 1JX, England
☎ 01993 812500
☎ +44 1993 812500

www.writersworld.co.uk

The text pages of this book are produced via an independent certification process that ensures the trees from which the paper is produced come from well managed sources that exclude the risk of using illegally logged timber while leaving options to use post-consumer recycled paper as well.

To David and Frances.

The best fruits of all my labours.

INTRODUCTION

If anyone had told me when I was twenty that forty years later I would find myself in a world of no pensions to speak of and where most of us would have to work for our whole lives, I would have thought we were royally fucked.

Which in a way we are. But in a good way.

Because as luck would have it, being fucked can be quite good fun.

You are, whether you realise it or not, living in an extraordinary time. You are right at the start of a revolution in the way women — and men — will work and live.

On the one hand, the expectations of the last 100 years are falling away: life expectancy and health are increasing almost exponentially; industries are being born and are dying at an unprecedented rate; some of the most highly sought after jobs today didn't even exist a decade ago; pensions and retirement are all but gone and won't be coming back.

More and more women will support themselves, and often their families, for most, if not all, of their lives.

Royally fucked? On the contrary, if we do it right, we will have the time, the energy and the opportunity to be a wide variety of things throughout our lives; to change careers, jobs, find new talents and explore what we can be.

This book is about where we are now and where we are going — in our personal lives and our work lives — as women in the 21st Century.

Women are, I believe, uniquely placed to take huge advantage of these inevitable changes. Barely a century ago, a woman as sole or main provider for herself or her family was unheard of, and it's our relative newness to the workplace which means we are much less resistant to change in our working lives than men. In fact, most of us are rightly still in discussion with ourselves about how to 'do' work as a female. The 'women at work' conversation is as vigorous now as it was in the late 60s when I entered the fray, and just when we might have expected to be getting a handle on it, the territory has shifted again.

The current 'crisis' is an incredible opportunity to rise above trying to work out how to negotiate with the modern workplace, with all its embedded prejudices and challenges, and to create a new one altogether. One that works for us, for the whole of our lives and through all of our personal incarnations as daughters, mothers, lovers, single women, parents, wives, divorcees, carers and widows.

And, as part of our good fortune, we are, unlike earlier generations, in control of our sex lives: reproduction, health, pleasure — we now get to call the shots. We are more aware, more comfortable and more eloquent (often pretty rudely eloquent) about sex than ever before. And that has given us a language and set of metaphors and imagery about sex that runs through our lives like a thread.

The Kama Sutra of Work uses that to a new end — to create hooks and triggers to help us create pleasure and security for ourselves via our work, paid or unpaid.

It starts by helping you see how many more talents you have than you ever thought. It then looks at how to get the very best out of work in any situation. It will take the lid off the myth of a 'job', and open your mind to what 'work' really means in the new world — and show you how to take advantage of opportunities you've never thought of as possible for you. You'll learn how to find and create work for yourself that fits where you are in your life at any point in time. And, on the way to this orgasmically satisfying and fulfilling work life, it'll equip you to deal with all those annoying little problems we often find in the workplace.

It's worked for me. It so happens that my working life has ended up as self-employed. But I got here relatively late in life via a series of employed jobs and other work and interests. I'm having more fun — and making more money — than at any point in my life.

My mother — who would by now have been 106 years old — used to say 'Never let a man buy you a house or a car'. If you find your knight in shining armour and live happily ever after, that's great, but it's a bit out of your control.

How much better is it to know that you can be all you were meant be: independent, secure and fulfilled, no matter what?

And, as luck would have it, it's sex that will help us do it.

So let's get started.

CHAPTERS

THE PROPOSITION

I have a proposition for you.

If you could use sex to make you happier and to make you more money at work, would you?

Obviously I don't mean shagging the boss or abusing your staff.

But, between the business of bed and the business of business, there's not much difference.

The world has changed and will change more.

You need to do work, and to live your life, differently.

So, if you're thinking about, having, or can remember ever having had sex, this book is for you. Because, frankly, women can be very frank about sex. And our intimacy with the language and imagery of sex gives us a great tool.

The Kama Sutra of Work will show you how to make the most of your talents, make more money and have more freedom — by hard-wiring what you do at work to your libido.

So, big swallow, are you ready?

CAUTION!
WOMEN AT WORK

Life is about being all we can be. It's about stretching ourselves, achieving things, falling down, getting up. It's about love and laughter, tears and fears.

And much of that we do through our work. Whether it's paid or unpaid, in or out of the home, what we were trained to do or fell into by chance — what we work at is what gives us our confidence, our independence and secures our future.

But, for the last few decades, society has paid an awful lot more attention to our sex lives than our work lives.

You can't escape sex. It's on a billboard near you, on your TV, in your magazines, at work, at home (maybe, maybe not...)

You are swimming in a sea of sexual language and imagery.

Sex dominates all other topics. Sex sells. It sells to you, all the time.

Seems a shame to let all that go to waste...

TALKING DIRTY

So, let's talk about sex shall we? After all, it's hardly the taboo topic of the Victorians (who, by the way, were shagging themselves senseless behind closed doors even whilst they were banning books right, left and centre). The thing about sex is that you just can't ignore it.

Sex is fun and playful and meaningful and messy and tender and funny and life-enhancing and excruciatingly embarrassing — sometimes all at once. And, whatever you think you know about it, it is not reserved for the young and beautiful.

There's good sex and bad sex — some is a matter of opinion and personal taste and some is a matter of fact. It is an all-absorbing topic of interest, fascination, and comment.

But, there is an upside to being drowned in a metaphorical sea of semen.

Because there I was, thinking about work and women, and about how to help women craft better work lives for themselves.

You see, work is very, very important to women. It gives us independence, security and freedom. It's often in work that we find our self-confidence and self-esteem. In practical terms, we need to be able to work to cope with life and all it throws at us. It helps us find our talents, grow our skills, and give ourselves pleasure.

Oh hello...

Work allows women to give themselves pleasure.

Erm, that sounds peculiarly like sex to me.

Now, I am of the era of *The Joy of Sex*. That was the book that started the revolution, along with the Kinsey Report (précis — women like sex too) and the Pill. *The Joy of Sex* had illustrations (no photos, that would have been PORN) of a very hairy, bearded man and his long-haired lover. The illustrations alone served as a useful contraceptive.

Later came *Cosmopolitan* magazine, *Forum*, *Readers' Wives*, *Sex and the City*, Brazilian waxes, boob jobs, vajazzles (WTF?) and all the rest, and what have we got? A generation of women who have been taught and bombarded so much that they often know more about sex than they do about work. Who are entirely at ease in calling the shots in their sex lives — and not so capable of calling the shots at work.

Well Avril, I thought, you've got to be able to do something with that.

2

TOP SHELF

As I so often do when I've had a 'light-bulb' moment, I turned to my overstocked bookshelves to try and figure out how best to talk to women in a way that would be useful and entertaining.

And sticky — as in you'd remember it. (But of course, now my brain was in that direction, all I could think of was *Sticky Fingers* — thank you Rolling Stones.)

And there, nestled on a shelf in the corner between the *Secret Garden* and *Galileo's Daughter* (my tastes are nothing if not catholic) was *The Kama Sutra*.

The Richard Burton translation, written in 1883, bought in 1983.

I flicked through the book and, to my surprise, it contained not a single illustration. Not even one little suggestive line drawing. No wonder it had stayed unread for three decades. I probably only bought it for the pictures.

I was, to say the least, disappointed.

But, oh my word! When I started reading, it hit the spot. And lit the fire.

As one would expect of *The Kama Sutra*.

3

BETWEEN THE SHEETS

Convinced as I am that intuition is rarely wrong, I persevered: drawings or no drawings. And at Chapter Three all the gods conspired to make me smile.

In it, a woman was advised to learn the sixty four (!) sexual practices from a trusted female friend. (Fair enough. I guess it's not the kind of thing you could go to college for.)

But, she was then advised, and I am being selective here for the list was long, to also become proficient in the following:

Singing... Dancing... Writing and drawing... Culinary arts...

No surprises there then. But wait...

Foreign languages and dialects…

And…

Carpentry, chemistry and mineralogy, knowledge of mines and quarries...

And I kid you not...

Code-breaking.

And the reason for this advice?

I quote:

> *"If a wife becomes separated from her husband, and falls into distress, she can support herself easily, even in a foreign country, by means of her knowledge of these arts."*

Even *The Kama Sutra*, centuries ago, recognised the need for a women to be financially self-sufficient!

Lots of jobs. And not a blow job amongst them.

And I thought, "Maybe I'm onto something here…"

FIND YOUR G SPOT(S)

Pleasure is a great thing. The 'Kama' bit of The Kama Sutra means sensual pleasure. But of course we can get pleasure from all sorts of things: a lover's touch, a baby's smile, winning a race, overcoming adversity, a warm summer's day... the list is endless and very, very personal.

You are unique. What gives you pleasure is unique to you and it's in those things that you will find your flow. And it's in your flow that you create the person you were meant to be.

'Sutra' simply means a little saying to help you sum up and remember something — like 'Breast is best'.

The 'Sutras' you will find here are the elements that make up the thread of how you find — and stay in — your flow.

Because when something makes you happy, it's easy to persevere at it.

When you know you will eventually get pleasure, you put some effort in. Or you'll at least start.

But sometimes you have to get deep inside yourself to find out what feels good...

RUSSIAN DOLLS

The Mandarin Oriental on a Friday night. A bar full of breathtakingly beautiful women draped over equally breathtakingly unappealing men. Who are very rich. It's a career, of sorts. In the short-term perhaps lucrative, but not what you'd bring your daughters up to do.

I hate making sweeping generalisations, especially about the supposed differences between men and women. I spent most of my early decades angrily denying any gender behavioural differences.

But hey, we all know women can change their minds.

Men tend to run their lives in a linear fashion. They move from item to item in their heads sequentially. They compartmentalise things. Relationships, work and tasks tend to be dealt with one at a time. This can make them simultaneously very effective — and very irritating.

Women on the other hand weave together all the elements of their lives. They transport thought patterns, skills and learned behaviours across invisible boundaries in their personal, family and work lives. This can make them simultaneously very effective — and very irritating.

The Russian dolls in The Mandarin Oriental will move on to new careers when they've banked enough cash.

But they give us a much better analogy than considering being a hooker as a career move.

All of us, men and women, have many more talents than we know. We die never knowing what we could have been because they are left unexplored. This was even more the case in the past when lives were typically short and hard.

Now, however, we live longer, much longer. And although you might not be aware of it, the changing economy of the world means that more and more of us have a chance to explore our latent gifts and talents over the course of long working lives.

Which means that we can be more than one thing, very often all at the same time. And I don't just mean a daughter, sister, aunt, mother, friend, colleague — all those wonderful and critical personal relationships that women build as a matter of course.

We can unpack our Russian dolls and find that we can be an engineer, a mother, a physics teacher, a businesswoman, a financial adviser, a coach, a therapist, a business adviser, a writer... and who knows what else?

That lot above, that's me. From 1973 to now, that's how I have earned, and do earn, money.

You are sitting on a mine of untapped talent, a rich seam of potential. Cool, huh?

SUTRA: Recognise that there is more, much more, to you than meets the eye.

5

TURN ONS

Elegant hands and wrists. A gorgeous body wrapped in a sharp suit. A white V-neck T-shirt. Not knowing he's sexy. A sprinkling of grey. A scarily bright brain and slightly short fuse. These things are turn-ons for me — amongst other things.

Being turned on is amazing. A frisson of pleasure and anticipation. That visceral attraction, inexplicable and unexpected, is what finds people head over heels in love.

And when it's not there, nothing, no amount of money, looks, charm or charisma can make it happen.

But, out of the blue, you can find yourself turned on by the short, bald guy with the self-deprecating sense of humour. It's Mr Big vs. Harry in *Sex and the City*. A '*coup de foudre*' and there you are, hit by passion and your 'list' goes out of the window.

Turn ons are things that cause emotions. And emotions make us happy or sad, smile or frown, lighter or heavier, tingle or not. Turn offs, well, they turn us off. The absence of passion is as tangible — and as heavy — as the euphoria of passion is breathtakingly light.

The secret is to recognise it. In affairs of the heart and the body, it's pretty easy. Less so in work, if only because for many of us, we don't expect to find it there.

But you need to.

Do you know what it feels like to be turned on at work? To really be absorbed in something that captures your attention, makes time fly, takes your breath away? Or to see someone doing something and think, 'I want to do that!'

It can be small or big. It can be life-changing or mundane. Knitting a beautiful jumper or designing a ship. Making up bedtime stories for your kids or writing a novel. Coding a new game or clearing messy admin. What you love doing — and you can and will love many different things — is unique to you.

Start paying attention to what you like. Watch for when you get a rush of pleasure. Don't analyse how or if you might make money, or a career, out of it. That's like assessing a man for husband potential on the first date. Always scary (especially for him because men can smell that) — and usually wrong.

We fail to recognise that pleasure is designed to give us clues as well as goose bumps. Pleasure lets us see inside ourselves, to what makes us tick.

We forget what we used to love.

Recently I met a very successful lawyer. She's fifty three and is thinking she wants to change her life and career. In the middle of our conversation, she blurted out she simply doesn't know how she ended up as a lawyer. She sort of sleep-walked into it to please her Greek parents. What she really wants to do is write about Eastern European history and culture. As a child, she was obsessed with it, amassing books and memorabilia.

As it happens she's made enough money that she can go off and do that now. But what if she pops her clogs next week? It will have been a life spent living someone else's ambitions, a spirit dampened and a talent withered.

Make a point of staying aware of pleasure, interest and fascination. It's a muscle you've probably let waste a bit. You need to exercise it.

SUTRA: What turns you on makes you tick.

MASTURBATION

But what if you really don't know what turns you on, and you're so out of practice you don't know where to start?

You know how sometimes you want your man to be psychic? To somehow know what you want, when you want it. Like in *Avenue Q* when the puppet shouts to her lover: "Left a bit. Left, LEFT!" Then, a moment later, "Not your left, MY left!"

Well. You're like that with yourself, almost certainly. Not entirely sure what flicks your switches — until it happens. Which leaves an awful lot of wonderful, pleasure-giving possibilities as just that — possible but not probable.

Learning what you like means getting out of your comfort zone. After all, you know what you know and that's all that you know. It takes more than one attempt to get spinach down the average two-year-old's throat if he has not been exposed to it early enough.

So, you have to make an effort to expose yourself to new things.

Practice being flexible so that your brain learns to be flexible and open to newness.

You can nudge this along in the most mundane elements of your day. Go to work a different way. Buy lunch in a new place each day. Look up at the tops of buildings, not down at the pavement. Trivial changes in routine loosen up the straightjacket around your brain and feelings.

Try a new activity. Do something a little scary. Extending just one bit of your comfort zone spreads like a virus to the whole of your life. You can't be a little bit brave just like you can't be a little bit pregnant.

Remember what you used to like when you were a kid. Try it out again. The lawyer who wanted to study history knew that when she was young and she knows it still.

What? It feels impractical to still want to be a rock star when you're pushing sixty? Tell that to my friend Martin who has just released his second self-penned album. Has it made him money directly? No. Has it made him that rarest of animals: a creative accountant (not that kind of creative accountant)? Hell yeah. And he gets new clients and work because of it.

At work, offer to do something you've never done before. Ask to be shown how someone else does their work.

Volunteer somewhere just to see what it's like.

Ask people to tell you what you're good at, then see if it's what you actually like doing. Because the two are not always the same. I, for instance, am pretty damned good at operational stuff. People pay me a lot of money to do it. I hate it.

Watch when other people are obviously turned on by what they do. How do they walk, talk, and present themselves? Store away what it looks like. Then you might notice when it happens to you. Finding your G- spot is about practice.

And lastly, do you know how a marketing guy in the 1970s doubled the sales of a shampoo almost overnight with just three words? He simply had the manufacturers put on the instructions on the back of the bottle 'Rinse and repeat'.

You need to keep rinsing and repeating all through your life. To identify the thing you've kept doing but shouldn't have and to dig out the wonderful new things you haven't yet encountered or noticed.

SUTRA: Make discovering what pleasures you a habit. It won't make you blind. It'll open your eyes. Rinse and repeat.

EXPLORATION

Lady Chatterley's Lover, The Secret Garden, Fifty Shades of Grey.

Erotic fiction has a huge market. We read it partly to excite and stimulate and partly to learn. We are curious about sex. Especially curious sex.

I've found myself reading erotic fiction and noticed that my head has tilted to the side whilst my imagination tries to work out how THAT works. We create pictures in our heads — in fact, getting the right mental picture is the key to heightened arousal. Once we get the one that hits our buttons, we're off to the races, so to speak.

And there are numerous reports of rekindled sex lives after women have read stuff that sparked their imagination, that maybe they had simply not thought of trying before. Or had done before but got out of the habit of doing. Imagination can turn into reality pretty damn fast if you've got enough incentive — or just the plain, raging horn.

But what about your work life? Is there a work equivalent of *Fifty Shades of Grey*? Well, yes, it's called the rest of the world.

The business of knowing what is going on in the world, what you don't know, what other people know and do that you don't, is essential. Research it. Be curious.

You probably don't know a fraction of the types of jobs people are doing now. You don't know which markets are dying and which are being born.

Many businesses start with no cash and deliberately stay small. Traditional industries are being pushed to the wall as more people use the Internet to go small and quirky or do it themselves — better, faster and cheaper.

You can become a star from your bedroom on YouTube.

You don't know what has gone out of favour but will come back (vinyl records).

Or what looked like it was going to take over the world but didn't (e-readers).

In the 80s, everyone thought the cinema would die as people got their own DVD players. Nope.

And if you can save, make or convert energy, you're onto a winner in a country where we only have about three days' energy supply at any one time.

Your future work will depend a lot on how much you are swimming in the actual river, not just standing on the bank watching it pass.

You need to self-educate. Start to notice trends. Dig into stuff you seriously don't know anything about. Find people and talk to them. But most of all *listen*.

Know what's happening in the world.

Set yourself a regime of reading (or watching) widely and well. Go to lectures, don't just go online. Turn up. Meet like-minded, curious people. Get into TED talks, podcasts, The School of Life. Saturate your spare time with ideas outside of your knowledge. Don't discriminate. Just expose yourself to stimulation.

SUTRA: Stay alert and keep your antennae up. Notice the tingle. Because love is all around you. (Starts humming gently...)

AIM FOR THE CLIMAX

When you settle in your sex and love life, you are heading for disaster. You make a decision that you will forego what you really want in case what's on offer now is all you're going to get.

You do it, if you do it at all, for a whole host of reasons: you think you're not worthy of something better; you're lonely and anyone is better than no one; you think time is running out.

None of those is true. Not one.

And any short-term relief you get is negligible compared to years of dissatisfaction until you either pull the plug or get so numb you accept your 'fate'.

Translate that into work and you are throwing your very essence away.

It is through the work you do that you will find the best you, and that work is going to come in all sorts of different forms. Many of those forms you don't even know about or certainly have never contemplated for yourself. You simply don't know what wonderful things are out there, waiting for you to discover them.

You have a superpower. The power of choice. If you were born in the western world you get more ability to exercise that choice than many other women worldwide.

So, why would you choose to settle for anything other than the best for yourself?

KEEPING IT UP

Your standards, that is.

Ladies, ladies. I can't stress this enough. You will attract precisely what you think you deserve. No more, no less.

That chubby loser with no ambition who brings you garage flowers? Yep, poor, sweaty little Derek. You ordered him up. The guys who never call you when they say they will? Them too.

The Cross Channel ferry lover (roll on-roll off)? And him (he does seem to get about a lot).

The crap job with the boss who never notices you? Yep. The lower pay than the six blokes in your department? I know it's illegal but it happens (especially in finance, ironically. There they seem to intuitively know that how you value your employees can be demonstrated in cold, hard cash. So when they pay you less, you know what they're telling you, don't you?)

This is the bit that no one wants to accept. You get what you expect to get, deep down. You can mouth off all you want about how you won't take shit from anyone but then you do and it's game over.

You need standards and you need to start with you.

Do not ask anyone to do anything you won't do.

Do not do anything you would not ask your daughter/sister/mother/best friend to do.

Do not do or go along with anything your employers wouldn't ask a man to do.

Be polite but firm.

Be punctual and groomed — and get over yourself if you think that's sexist. It isn't. Looking good is good manners. I expect it of men and women.

Be well informed, well read and researched. Be prepared, Girl Guide or not.

Do NOT be ditzy or girlie. You are a woman, not a child.

Demand to be paid well, treated well and fairly.

BUT, strident is not good. Practice control. Stay measured. Be precisely what you admire most.

Decide what your standards are and stick to them. And accept that your standards are not to everyone's taste.

After all, you don't have to go to bed with the guy with bad breath, do you?

SUTRA: Be prepared not to settle for less than you deserve.

A GIRL'S BEST FRIEND

Not diamonds. Sorry. Although I am partial to a carat or six and they can at least be hawked if push comes to shove. In other words, they're valuable. But not as valuable as your values.

Derek is a reflection of something inside of you. And not just that you seem to sell yourself short.

When you pick up the call from the guy who didn't get in touch for weeks, when you succumb for the second (third, fourth...) time to the crap lover, you're getting big flashing (non orgasmic) signals about what drives you. And it's not good.

I know a guy, let's call him Tony. Tony is on a dating website. Actually he's on several. He has a routine which involves a bit of fast flirting, followed by a swift move to a meeting, and the 'romantic' kill and then disappearing. So far, so normal.

A couple of weeks pass and then he reappears. He plays a clever numbers game, working on the principle that if he charmingly asks enough women for a shag, someone is bound to say yes.

What makes it funny (and sad) is that he recently contacted two people I know with identical 'fishing expedition' messages. *"Darling! Morning — I woke with the most gorgeous sensual dreams... I was enveloped in the sheerest softest silk, with long lingering kisses... did you visit me in my sleep...? Shall we meet over the wknd..."*

And sometimes it will work, although all it did on this occasion was to give three women an evening of unbridled hysteria and tears of laughter rather than passion. To be fair, that can be better than sex sometimes — thanks Tony.

But, what does this tell us? It tells us that we all have things that really matter to us, that drive our behaviour. They are our values.

Some people value money more than anything. Others value friendship, or love, or contribution, or sex, or just company. And Tony knows that. In this context, Tony values getting laid. But he positions himself to appeal to a woman who is looking for affection too, which most of us are.

We all have a hierarchy of values and that list will drive what we do in life and the choices we make. It will drive you to decisions and worries, and it will drive you mad if you try to go against it. You might always go for money first. Or you might go for power, or position — especially if you've been taught that money doesn't make you happy, as I was.

You might value being told how clever or good you are.

Your values are a reflection of your inner self-esteem and the way you were brought up, the beliefs you hold about yourself and the world.

But because of the way society values things, too many of us have forgotten that we have our own personal value systems.

Screw what anyone else thinks. Be a stay at home mum, be a driven career woman, be a drifter. But check in with yourself to make sure that whatever you are doing really fits your value system, whilst you are growing as a person.

And check that your value system is still valid and on your side from time to time! Because sometimes we end up living by values we were taught that don't help us any more.

And it's only when your value system has sorted itself out via healthy self-esteem and a bit of internal hard work that you will find you make, and stay at ease with, choices that truly resonate with your core.

I never used to value money — in that I felt it wasn't a good thing to aim for in life. I was brought up to value hard work, putting others first and being respected. I was taught that money simply didn't make you happy. Maybe not, but now I know it can buy you a big enough yacht to sail right up to it. So now I make enough money as well as doing all the other things that matter to me.

SUTRA: Pay attention to your values. They are the outer signals of your inner life. You will see them in what you do, not what you say.

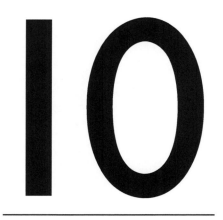

SELF LOVE

Now then, assuming that you eschew Derek and his undesirable mates, how do you go about attracting a fabulous, gorgeous lover and have fabulous, amazing sex?

After all, we know that you've looked at your standards — handsome, at least to you, tick; kind, tick; funny, tick (I know, but it's true, women like funny men and really can be laughed into bed); solvent, tick — add in whatever matters to you, no one is judging you.

You've pretty much worked out what your values are and they're solid and helpful.

So it's only a matter of time then till we bag Mr Sex on Legs, isn't it?

Not quite; we have one missing component. You.

I know this is hard, but someone has to tell you.

You are not perfect. Not even close.

All those books that tell you to love yourself as you are? I'm not buying that.

Love yourself, for sure, love the core of you. Love what you can and will be.

Here's the thing. Love is a hard word. A big word. A HUGE word. True love is unconditional. The closest human form is that of a parent for a child. And even then, you can love your child so much your heart could burst but still not really like them very much sometimes.

And it's the same with you. Love yourself to bits — that's an order — but also work on the bits that you don't like and that you see don't serve you well. You've got to know what you need to change to be the better you. Peel back the layers and dig up the drains. Be like an athlete and know that the muscles have to be torn to grow stronger.

Recognise your faults. (And, no, being ten pounds heavier than you want to be, having a nose marginally bigger or boobs slightly smaller than what you think would be perfect, they're not faults. They are the result of media propaganda. Do not buy into this shit. That's an order too!)

A lack of discipline, low self-esteem and confidence, emotional incontinence, a failure to take responsibility for yourself — these are real faults that damage you, and the minute you accept them you fail yourself.

You are here to grow, develop, become the person you are at the very core of you — glowing, trail-blazing and wonderful.

Work like a bastard (and I speak as one who actually *is* illegitimate so I feel allowed to use the term) to be better, stronger, kinder. Never, *ever* settle for the propaganda that says mediocre is fine, average is acceptable, coasting is good.

The biggest, hardest work you need to do is on you: your relationships, your health, your friendships, your family, your discipline, your interests, your sports, your hobbies. You know it's working when you notice one day that you are more — bigger — than you were yesterday or last week. (And that Krispy Cremes were not involved)

And then give yourself a hug. Inside.

SUTRA: Love yourself enough to be brutally truthful to yourself.

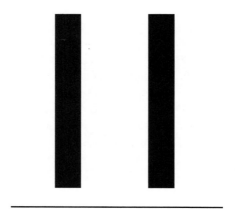

COMING FIRST

Ooh, sexual etiquette. Interesting.

Personally I think that a man should always treat a woman well; holding doors, walking on the outside of the pavement and putting her first sometimes. Old-fashioned it may be but I see no conflict in being both a feminist and a woman who rather loves a strong, respectful man. These gentle courtesies, plus doing nice things for my man — and putting him first at times too — are what oil the wheels of a human relationship.

But sometimes it really is necessary to put yourself first.

In bed, it's always good to be sure that you won't be left, frustrated as hell, staring at the ceiling whilst he falls into a post-orgasmic snooze.

So yes, in the main, coming first is not only good, it's often the only way it's likely to happen at all without a bit of DIY. No woman worth her salt puts up with a selfish lover.

But in life generally and at work?

I once presented to an audience of mainly middle-aged women. The subject of the day was recreating life after the nest emptied. Of course, increasingly the little birds come back home again these days and unless you move home secretly in the night without telling them, you never get rid.

But for this group, they were standing on the edge of perhaps another forty or fifty years with absolutely no idea of what to do with themselves.

And when I said I wanted them to put themselves first, you would have thought I'd asked them to lightly broil and eat their own children. Because an awful lot of women put everyone else first. Kids, parents, family, partners. Even bloody pets. Apparently it's what women are for.

My arse.

I'm all for being kind, helpful and generous. And people know that. Probably the way they know that about you. So when they ask you to do something you say 'yes' before you think.

You stay late for the third night in a row to do a presentation for a colleague because she's stressed. Obviously you don't get stressed. Ever.

You go to an unscheduled business meeting for a client when you really need to be at a prospect meeting for yourself. So the client gets away with being demanding and disorganised and you assume greater risk of trying to find new work.

You can't work out how to get to the gym because who'll walk the dog? Because of course everyone in your house has far more important things to do.

And you think you are doing them a favour. You're not. You are indulging their weaknesses and stopping them taking responsibility for themselves.

You will be told your reward is in Heaven.

But it isn't. Heaven is waiting, on Earth, for the woman who helps those who cannot help themselves, not the ones that need a sharp kick up the backside. Heaven on Earth is waiting for the one who looks after her health and well-being so that she is a beacon of energy and enthusiasm to the people around her. Who knows that unless she looks after herself she is no bloody good to anyone else. And who knows that when she ends up not where she wanted to be, no-one is going to listen to her whingeing about being taken for granted.

As they say on airlines — 'Put on your own oxygen mask first.'

Then you can bugger off and be a hero if you want.

SUTRA: Tough love works. Do it.

FILTHY LUCRE

In the business of sex, money is a pretty fluid notion. It's the case that Derek may have paid for sex at some time — either directly or via an awful lot of dinners and drinks out.

Filthy lucre in this case means good hard cash but it can just as easily be any number of methods of payment. And it can vary wildly depending on the circumstances. For example, our Russian dolls in the Mandarin Oriental don't charge the same as the girl at King's Cross.

Who makes up the rules about money? We do. And often we do it badly.

Too many women talk about money like it's the enemy. The root of all evil (wrong quote, of course). Money doesn't buy you happiness, they say. It doesn't, but it's better and easier to be well off and miserable than poor and miserable, surely?

Money is not dirty. Money is utterly without a value system (and, no, I am not talking about bankers).

Also known as currency, money is simply a universal exchange mechanism. Like a cow for some beans. Now if you didn't happen to have a cow but wanted some beans, money would be jolly handy.

We women, and I include myself, are notoriously rubbish at being paid our worth. Even with the apparent laws about equality of the sexes, we get paid less, often because we ask for less. Or do more for the same money.

I believe in really working hard and giving more than value for money to anyone who pays me. But when it comes to the financial equivalent of rape and pillage, which is what often happens when a woman does not negotiate well for herself, I draw the line.

If you're bad at asking to be paid, start with barter instead. Exchange your ability to code break for a year's supply of Pinot Grigio. Whatever you want. Just make it an exchange that you consider fair.

Once you've got the hang of bartering, move onto bucks.

If all else fails, get someone else to negotiate for you. I see nothing wrong with outsourcing my weaknesses. If Adele — no shrinking violet — uses an agent, I'm damn sure I can.

And, no, I am not saying never do anything for nothing. Of course we ought to give of ourselves to others. Charity work, volunteering, helping someone in need — they all form a crucial part of healthy emotional lives and strong communities.

Just don't get turned over. Compare yourself logically to what a (good, capable) man would be paid for what you intend to do. Add 20% and negotiate down only if you have to.

People will pay you what *you* think you're worth, not just what they think you're worth.

SUTRA: Money is a measure. How do you measure up?

TRICKS OF THE TRADE

They say that Mrs Simpson — the woman who seduced and married a King, had learned exotic sexual techniques in the Far East. The mind boggles.

But there's no doubt that a little bit of technique never hurt anyone. There are things that you do on a daily basis that, if you did them just a little better you might get further, faster.

And there's nothing better than knowing you're using all your assets well.

After all, if you're aiming at creating an orgasmic life, a few tricks never did anyone any harm, did they?

13

ORAL

Mouths are great things. The largest concentration of nerve receptors in the body.

They can do so much more than talk. Or eat.

Lips, tongues, even teeth — they can give us, and others, such amazing sensations.

Lord knows, just the mention of oral will stop most guys in their tracks.

So let's give them some more. And not just the men. This is not a time to discriminate.

So, a question. How much oral do you do?

Do you speak up when you think you're being overlooked?

Do you join in a discussion when you have something to add?

Do you ask for what you want at work?

I doubt it. We aren't particularly good at that, us women. It's curious how we have no qualms demanding satisfaction in bed but can't ask for a pay rise or get our opinion heard.

I have lost count of the number of times when a woman has come up to me after a meeting to raise a very valid point that she could, and should, have raised in the meeting.

Not because they are worried that they might be asking a silly question. Generally, women don't mind doing that as much as men. Men can be reluctant to admit ignorance, women less so usually. Often when I stop a meeting to ask for clarification, suddenly my male colleagues will be nodding along like a row of plastic dogs on a car shelf. One great upside of having less testosterone is that we don't have to protect our balls every time we feel under threat.

No, women are asking themselves: 'Do I know enough about this to contribute anything at all?'

You know what, if you're in the room you know enough.

You HAVE to ask for what you want. You HAVE to tell people what you can do. You HAVE to speak up if you are being overlooked.

Because if you don't, you make yourself a victim.

Because if you don't, you expect that everyone else should somehow, magically, know what is going on in your head.

Because if you don't, you betray all the women out there in the world, who are not even *allowed* to speak up.

Because you are your own CEO and YOU are in charge of your life.

Speaking up doesn't mean becoming strident or stroppy. You can still be charming, feminine and kind — and proffer your opinions at work. The two are not mutually exclusive.

SUTRA: Give great oral. People will respect you for it.

DOWN A BIT, LEFT A BIT...

Sometimes we have a habit of expecting people to read our minds. We do this especially with men, even more so with men we are supposed to love.

For example, in bed, we often think he should just KNOW what feels good and what doesn't. Telling him would seem like, well, letting him off the hook.

And when a man fails to notice that something is bothering us, we prefer it if they work it out through an elaborate charade of guesswork. 'If you don't know, then I'm certainly not going to tell you.'

Think about all this for a moment. If your fourteen-year-old behaved like that, what would you do? Personally I'd tell them to go away and grow up.

Which is precisely what women need to do. There is NOTHING embarrassing or stupid about being 100%, entirely clear, about what you want and then saying it. Snuffling round the edges, hoping that someone will pick up the hint, is like playing blind man's bluff in the dark with mittens on.

When you need to tell someone at work that the way you are being treated isn't fair, be forensic about it. Not moaning, just clinically and factually correct.

If you want to be able to do something or be given a chance, articulate your reason for believing you can, outline the benefits to them of you trying and, even more, the benefits to them of you succeeding.

You see, although I insist that we act like grown-ups, on occasion it works best if we assume that we are working with small children. Speak slowly, calmly, clearly and unemotionally with the underlying assumption that, of course, they will agree with us.

They just had to have it explained.

SUTRA: Be clear, calm and candid.

15

LUBRICATION

Lube. KY. Wet and Wild. Love Honey.

Lubrication makes everything so much easier.

Without it things can get uncomfortable, possibly even intolerable. Of course, the best kind is natural lubrication, if you get my drift. But natural or artificial, lubrication leads to more pleasure, more easily and usually more often.

I can say with certainty that lubrication is also the single biggest contributor to my satisfaction. At work.

I got into lube in a big way when I was way, way younger and less confident. I hated being thrust into rooms full of strangers and trying to make conversation. So, like a cat bringing home a mouse, I would immediately try to work out how I could engage whoever I was talking to. I would find out all I could about them (and trust me, if you are ever lost for words, just let people talk about themselves. They'll come away thinking you were the most interesting person in the room), and then I would go through my mental file to see who they should be talking to/meeting or give them an idea or piece of information — or sometimes just encouragement. And then I would remember to get back to them with an introduction or information.

It was only years later I worked out that my huge network came from this little tactic to avoid feeling like a lemon.

If you are going to build your net worth, the one thing you need is a network.

And let's get one thing straight. Networking is NOT turning up at an organised event every Tuesday at 7am and standing up for one minute to tell people what you do and why they should use you.

Nor is it carrying around a huge stack of business cards and distributing as many as you can to everyone you meet.

Or pouncing on every potential lead like a rat up a drainpipe (note similarity to desperate dating...)

It is not aggressive, selfish, intimidating or scary.

It is the most old-fashioned and genteel way of doing business. And it is based on a few assumptions:

1. You intend to be working for a long time therefore there is no rush.

2. You take a genuine interest in the other person, both work life and personal.

3. You want to know how to help the other person first.

4. You expect nothing in return but know that it will come back to you somewhere, sometime.

5. You make relationships with people you like. This is NON NEGOTIABLE. Quite apart from the fact that you are likely to fall out eventually if you don't like them, you may well get shafted too and that's not good for your soul. (See Buggery later)

Great lubrication is not about who has the most LinkedIn or Facebook contacts.

Great lubrication is when people start coming to you because they think you might know someone they need to speak to. Or they have an idea and wonder how you might help. Or they just know that you will hear them out. You would be astonished how many people really just need a good, hard listening to.

When I come towards the end of a contract, I can happily put out feelers to a dozen or so centres of influence who I know will help me out by keeping me at the front of their minds if they hear of anything. Effectively I employ a sales team for me.

And the only cost has been years and years of goodwill.

So get slippery.

SUTRA: Make everything so much easier and more comfortable. Lubricate like crazy.

16

YES! YES! YES!

Everyone knows that the single biggest turn on for a man is an enthusiastic woman. Pretty much any kind of woman but especially the one they happen to be in love with. Someone who is giving it their all — full attention, full commitment, full sense of adventure, fun and possibility. Totally in the moment.

I have a mantra.

I had it engraved on a ring, which I wear most of the time except when I want to get the bling out. It says, 'This too shall pass.'

It's there to remind me that everything, EVERYTHING, passes eventually. The awful worries either come to fruition or pass. Mainly they pass. We spend endless precious days, weeks, even years, worrying about stuff that never actually happens.

> "Worrying is as effective as trying to solve an algebra equation by chewing bubble gum. The real worries in your life are apt to be ones that never crossed your worried mind. The ones that blindside you on some idle Tuesday."

> Baz Luhrman

In the meantime, the amazing, happy moments pass, screeching past our ears before we even take time to notice them. Golden moments that should be engraved in our minds, treated shamefully, routinely and ungratefully.

Shit happens. OK, it's not original I know. But over the course of any given day stuff is going to happen. Good stuff, bad stuff, boring stuff. Sometimes it really does feel like every sodding day is the same as the one before and that all the ones coming might be the same too. Sometimes you feel out of control and subject to the vagaries of a very unhelpful and unkind fate. When everyone else seems to have a great job, a fabulous career, a gorgeous lover and a dazzling future.

At which point you can choose to either just sit in the middle of it like a lump of useless flotsam bobbing on an ocean of shit, or you can decide to take a nanosecond to realise that THIS IS IT. This is your life. This is now and you are NEVER going to get this moment back.

If you don't like it, work on changing it. If you can't work out how to change it right this minute, work on squeezing the pips out of it until you find something that makes it worthwhile.

Wherever you are, be there.

It really doesn't matter if you move on to new things or focus on where you are and make the most of it but do whatever you do with enthusiasm. It feels better inside for you and looks better outside to the people around you.

Because nothing in the world is so much fun, or so great to behold, as unbridled enthusiasm. And whatever you act out tends to become real in your life.

Drag out your inner Pollyanna. Jump about a bit. Get excited. Talk it up. Talk positively and batten down the hatches on negative comments. It's not American bullshit. It's not even bullshit.

Sometimes, even when you don't fancy it, you need to just have a go. Because you get in the mood by getting in the mood, and once you're in the mood... Well you know where I'm going with this...

SUTRA: Bring enthusiasm to everything even before you feel it. As the saying goes, "If you build it, they will come."

ALL FIRED UP

Enthusiasm takes energy though right? And sometimes you've just plain run out. And its hard to summon up the fire in your belly.

Like when you really can't be arsed any more with your difficult partner. So you stop doing the things that you used to do together or the things you used to do to please him or her. It's too much like hard work.

When you really don't fancy sex and he's just got into bed all showered and hopeful.

When only a headache will bring you joy tonight.

Interestingly, enthusiasm creates energy. This is one of those wonderful things about being human — we can so easily reverse our moods by reversing cause and effect.

It can happen by accident. I, for instance, can't stand being up very late. Midnight sees me drooping, if it sees me at all. Unless I find myself in the middle of a (usually) heated, interesting discussion with interesting, clever people. In which case I can stay up all night with the best of them.

That's why knowing what turns you on matters so much — because you will pursue those things with energy. You'll work longer, wake earlier, stay up later, to do what turns you on.

My all time favourite quote is from George Bernard Shaw:

> *"This is the true joy in life, the being used for a purpose recognized by yourself as a mighty one; the being thoroughly worn out before you are thrown on the scrap heap; the being a force of Nature instead of a feverish selfish little clod of ailments and grievances complaining that the world will not devote itself to making you happy."*

> *George Bernard Shaw,* Man and Superman, Epistle

Pay attention to that line — 'a purpose recognised by YOURSELF as a mighty one.'

Graffiti artist? Dog groomer? Fashionista? Doctor? Or all four at once?

Be true to yourself because that's where your energy will come from.

Recognise your energy as your most precious physical asset. Teach yourself how to know when your energy is flowing and when it isn't.

We all get the same number of hours in a day. The people who seem to get more than twenty-four hours work done in any day are fired up with energy that comes from their enthusiasm about something. They treat their day as precious, to be spent wisely and well. The energy comes.

I have one project that requires me to get up at 5am some days. Do I have trouble getting myself out of bed and into the shower? Never, because what I will end up doing more than compensates for the lost sleep.

And when, for my 59th birthday, my son ordered me to get healthy (by buying me a full year of personal training, no excuses accepted and no, I could not exchange it for a Chanel suit), I discovered that exercise really does give you more energy, not less. So, three times a week with a personal trainer continues two years later and I have more energy than ever before.

It's no coincidence that top level CEOs are often exercise enthusiasts. They know it energises them and reduces stress.

Add to that physical energy a focussed mind and a sense of purpose and you will be unstoppable.

Turn up to whatever you do with energy. Even the things you don't like but can't change — yet.

And energy suckers? Avoid them as if they carried the bubonic plague. They do, in an emotional sense. People in whose company you feel angry, sad, insecure, frightened — avoid them until you learn how to manage your emotions around them.

If you can't, stay away from them.

You have too many important things to do to be stopped by anyone.

SUTRA: Burn, baby, burn!

18

DOES MY BUM LOOK BIG IN THIS?

Anyone who has ever sucked her tummy in before getting into bed and avoided nudity with the lights on knows that body confidence matters.

Actually, to the man into whose bed you are climbing the actual state of your body is of little importance (within reason). Frankly, just being in bed with a naked woman and the possibility of sex is enough for most men.

Some people are confident and some aren't. Or are they? Is lack of self-confidence just another excuse for not getting to where you want to go? If so, you have to work on it and use every trick in the book.

Because confident women are gob-smackingly amazing.

Christine Lagarde facing down the Greek Prime Minister. Marie Colvin in an eye patch and a war zone. Helen Mirren in a red bikini (yes, it's fine to be confident about your looks).

(By the way, Google Christine Lagarde and the Greek — notice their body positioning. You don't need to hear a word to know what's going on there and who is calling the shots. And it's not him.)

True confidence is knowing that you are as good as the next person. That you can do what you apply yourself to do; learn what you determine to learn; recover from whatever knocked you back; be what you decide to be.

It's not handed on a plate (thanks Simon Cowell for making that seem a possibility). Even with talent, without hard work, no one gets anywhere long term.

It's not being jealous of others and thinking they got it easier than you. Because if they did, good for them. It might happen to you too one day.

But we all have confidence inside ourselves — even if it's just singing in the shower or dancing in the kitchen with Prince on LOUD (yes, Patsy, that's you).

And because we have to start somewhere, we can do it just through how we dress. Now, I say this at the risk of incurring the wrath of my fellow, but marginally more militant, feminists. (And, yes, I am a feminist. I rather think that if you are a woman and you expect to be allowed to do and say what men do and say, you are, ergo, a feminist.)

Listen, I don't care if you go to work in sackcloth and ashes, Vivienne Westwood couture or dressed like an aging punk with colour blindness. Just look like you did it deliberately. Whatever you might want to believe about how people make up their minds about you, believe that how you turn yourself out matters. If you look boring and neutral and careless, that's what people will think. Unless you're Mary Beard, in which case, you carry on.

Now SHE has confidence (and she also wears fuck-off shoes.)

SUTRA: Lack of confidence, playing small, is not cool. Play big and the stage will grow to accommodate you.

FAKING IT

It's not a good thing in sex, faking it. It kind of means that you and your partner are not talking about what works for both of you. In the end, it spells trouble because you either fake it forever and then you never get any real fun, or you accidentally bump into someone with whom you don't need to fake it, and then it's curtains for the other relationship.

Faking it can be a passion killer (as in you never get to get any passion).

So, in sex, faking it has no real upside. But now and again it can be handy if you just want to get to sleep...

In work, however, faking it is the spark plug that gets your confidence engine roaring.

And, as luck would have it, your body is where it starts. Which is cool, as we all have one of those.

You see, your mind is not where you start with building confidence. Your mind is full of a million chattering monkeys who are clamouring to tell you that you don't know how to do this, can't understand that, are not as good as her, haven't got enough experience for that role.

I know this because I have just taken a telephone call from a head-hunter telling me that I am short-listed for a Non Executive Director role that I would love to have. I am being called for interview, along with two retired CEOs of public companies and a City legend.

So, my monkeys are having a field day. They've not had this much fun since I decided to write a book. Or maybe the time I decided to enter a fifty-four mile hike over the Highlands of Scotland in twenty-four hours, when I had previously never walked more than fifteen miles on the flat.

Yes, my monkeys get a lot of practice.

Fortunately, all that hippy trippy stuff I learned a couple of decades ago, works. That, plus some good old-fashioned wisdom.

To get confident, you have to act like it first. Stand upright, chin up, make your gestures expansive, take up some room, breathe deeply and easily, lower your voice in tone and increase its energy and volume.

Men are born to do this. They sit, legs spread wide in cramped tube trains. They lean back in chairs with arms behind their heads. They lounge lazily with one leg propped on the table. And they're not just posturing (although of course they are posturing). They are making themselves feel confident. And that confidence, often faked, is what gets them heard. (And, yes, a lot of the time they're talking bollocks — but they're talking it with confidence.)

These moves are called 'power moves' and they are scientifically proven to work — on everyone. When women (and men) stand tall, raise their arms above their heads like an Olympian breasting the tape, their cortisol (stress) levels drop and their dopamine (happy) levels rise — in a matter of seconds. Mohammed Ali had it taped. All that poetry, dancing around and bigging himself up made him stronger and braver.

Your mind and body do not know they are two separate things. You smile when you are happy. And you can make yourself happier by smiling. Hold a pencil lengthways between your teeth when you are feeling down and grumpy. Your mood will lift simply by virtue of the fact that you have forced the corners of your mouth into the shape of a smile.

Hold it between your lips and feel the process reverse as you shape your face into a sad pout.

Turn that frown upside down.

SUTRA: Fake it until you become it.

ON TOP

On top is your control position. Speed, sensation, penetration — all controlled by you. Getting on top does however pose some challenges for the less confident amongst us.

We fret about what we look like. We worry what it looks like to the observer. In other words, we deny ourselves pleasure because we know we don't (most of us) look like Helen Hunt in *The Sessions*.

On the other hand, remember that whatever you think you look like or are now, in ten years time you will look back wistfully and wonder why you didn't realise you were beautiful, brave and still had the entire world before you. At any age, trust me, looking back 10 years makes you realise how much you took yourself for granted. You don't know how fabulous you are right now.

On the matter of on top, personally I don't like to give gravity its head, so to speak.

At work, however, on top is very liberating.

When did you last push yourself forward to be the boss, to take a risk? To lead a project, head up a team, start a venture, stop a pointless discussion and bring it back into focus?

When did you last actually speak up so that you got a chance to shine? Or flop. It doesn't matter which really. Not in the long run.

Succeed or fail, you won't die, even if you feel that you'd like to. You are never as important to your colleagues as you think and they will forget your blunders and mishaps — so you should too. They're banking on it so that you cut them some slack when it's their turn.

If it really terrifies you, you can practise being on top in all sorts of ways first. Tackle the unordered dish that just appeared on your restaurant bill. Send back the inferior pudding. (I assume there is such a thing as an inferior pudding?) Don't be chicken about going out on your own at night (and yes, be safe, but this is a very safe country so don't become a prisoner of *Daily Mail* hysteria). Online date. Go to things on your own. Mentor a younger (or older) person who needs a bit of confidence building. Because when you are brave for someone else, you get braver too. (The secret is that you can't stop yourself hearing your strong and confident words for them and your simple little subconscious mind believes all it hears.) That'll teach them monkeys.

When you do one little thing to expand your comfort zone, after a very short time the whole comfort zone expands in every area. It's the only time you are likely to be grateful that once you start growing, you really can't stop.

SUTRA: Get your head above the parapet and lead the charge.

I WILL SURVIVE

The future is exciting and challenging. Which means sometimes it's just a bit tough. Which is fine, because we are tougher.

Wherever we are in our lives, we are still negotiating how to be in sex and at work. Traditional roles have gone out of the window and now we're having to make up new ways of being — but not everyone is on the same page.

With no pre-written rule-book (thank God for that), we need to make up our own and tackle any uncertainty ourselves. Which really means we have to use everything that gets thrown at us to make us stronger.

Every now and again, even a woman has to man up.

That time is now.

HOW WAS IT FOR YOU?

You lie back in a post-orgasm, oxytocin-laden stupor and gaze languidly and hopefully at your new partner. You ask, in your most tender voice, "Was that good?"

This is the moment where you expect to be told that it/you/they were awesome. The best ever.

He looks at you, coaxes a little bit of hair from your face, stares into your eyes, then into the far distance and ponders for a bit. You think, "Bless, he's trying to find enough poetry in his soul to express how magnificent, how unique and world shattering that was."

So when he looks away, rolls out of bed, reaches for his jeans and throws, "Don't think we really click, do we?" over his shoulder on the way to the bathroom, it's a tad crushing. Of course it's not a tad crushing. It's excoriating. It's devastating.

You report back to your girlfriends over copious quantities of vodka, lime and soda (maybe your arse really was too big after all...?) and they, with all the precision of a wrecking ball, take apart his total unworthiness of your magnificence.

Clearly the man is wrong. Rubbish in bed. And rude. And probably gay. Most definitely gay.

But, what if...

Oh, holy moly, what if he was RIGHT?!!!!!!!!!!!!

Now, clearly today is not the day you are going to thank him for his honesty and ring him up to find out what went wrong. Oh no. Today you are planning to fly-post his miserable weasel face all over his local area with something bloody rude but not quite illegal written all over it. Today you plan to insinuate on Facebook that he has some issues in the bedroom. Today you... of course, you'll never do any of them because...

YOU ARE A GROWN UP.

And grown-ups can take the truth. They ask for it. They know when it's worth paying attention to and when it needs to be ignored. They feed off it. Maybe that's why it's called feedback.

The ability to take feedback and use it to get better sorts the men from the boys. Or the women from the girls.

Training yourself to evaluate and use feedback is essential. That means knowing when it is relevant and true and when it is spiteful or ignorant and needs to be ignored. The best way to find out is to take it to people who know you well and ask them to tell you honestly if they agree or not. Be prepared for it to hurt — at least at the start. Then you'll find you can absorb it and use it to get better. Remind yourself that athletes and musicians and singers depend on feedback to improve. They pay people to critique them for God's sake.

I have a friend, Sue, who was going through holiday snaps with her husband. At each one she complained about how she looked. Finally her husband said to her, "Susan, I don't know what you think you look like, but that's what you look like."

Unfortunately very few people give feedback well. Make sure you are one of them.

SUTRA: Ask for feedback. Evaluate and absorb. Improve.

22

SEX ORGANS

Now, life can be shit sometimes. I know.

Fortunately, unless you actually die, it never stays the same. Sometimes you just have to hang in there for a bit until whatever is going wrong passes, as it inevitably will.

But life is so much better if you feel good about yourself. So, although this section demands a book in of its own, which I will get round to sometime, here are a few words on things that can make you feel good.

Things that do not involve alcohol, cigarettes, drugs or sex, which is handy because sometimes you just can't get a drunken shag with George Clooney when you need it.

Quick bit of science. You have three brains. The oldest bit at the bottom just keeps you breathing and stuff like that. The middle bit is where your feelings and emotions live. It's got almond shaped bits behind each ear called amygdala that fire up when you get scared (or scare yourself). The outside, newest bit is where we do our rational thought. That's the bit that sorts us out from the rest of the animal kingdom and the lack of it is why cats can't play chess; that and the lack of opposable thumbs of course — they can't pick the pieces up.

Now when our amygdala get a scare (bank card doesn't work, pregnancy test comes back positive when it shouldn't, boss shouts, HR calls us for a 'meeting') it shuts down the access to our rational brain. Which explains why, when you've just lost it with your partner because he/she shrank your best jumper by trying to be helpful, it's only later you realise you turned into a screaming banshee. When you ask yourself, "What on earth was I thinking, reacting like that?" the answer is, you weren't thinking. You were feeling.

Your amygdala are the reason you find it hard to do new things, to take risks, to change old habits, to stick at going to the gym or eating better. You're not useless. You're human with a pair of saboteurs who get over-enthusiastic sometimes.

The best way past them is to tip-toe. Do very small changes but do them often. In no time your saboteurs will recognise the changes are not life threatening (and 'life' means your ego just as much as your body) and you'll find yourself doing more and more new stuff more easily. In Japan they call this *Kaizen*. I call it baby steps. Your amygdala don't care what you call it.

No rational thought is required. Just do tiny things that seem irrelevant. So, leave the last bite of your chocolate bar instead of trying not to eat it at all. Walk on the spot for two minutes in the morning. Write 100 words of the book and then get up from your desk. Next week up it by another tiny bit. Your amygdala are snoozing nicely. Before you know it you've recreated how you look at and feel about the things that scared you.

So much of what we've been taught about self-improvement is totally wrong. Do not buy into thinking you can't change. You can re-programme yourself.

SUTRA: Re-wire yourself by making tiny efforts every day towards the things you want to master.

23

PELVIC FLOORS

In the great scheme of things that women have to put up with, along with period pain, episiotomies, caesarean scars, and sagging boobs, the pesky pelvic floor is right up there as one of the biggest pains in the asses.

Just when your body has got over from bringing up the numerous babies you squeezed out of an unfeasibly small channel and you think you might just take running up again, it delivers the drip drip of urinary incontinence. WTF?

In every sense we got the rough end of the deal.

Getting down to pelvic floor exercises is as important is making sure your legs will hold you up.

But a weak pelvic floor doesn't kill you (dying of embarrassment doesn't count). And it can be made strong again.

Just like the rest of you.

Your confidence may get battered and go into hiding. *You can build it back.*

Your pride may take a hammering. *You can recreate yourself.*

Your heart may break. *It will heal and you will love again.*

Your courage may fail. *It's only in hiding, waiting for you to call it out.*

You may think you simply can't deal with ONE MORE FUCKING THING going wrong.

You're wrong. *You can and you WILL deal with each and every thing that life will throw at you.*

You can lose your job, your home, what you thought was supposed to be your future. *You can make it all back, and better. I did.*

You need your health, your family and your friends.

But most of all you need you. And this is where we women excel.

We are stronger than silk, which is FIVE TIMES stronger than steel.

SUTRA: We can weave our own lives, no matter what is thrown at us.

24

BALANCE MY ARSE

Tiny touch of the *Eats, Shoots, and Leaves* there I'm afraid.

It should read 'Balance, my arse'. But I thought it was funnier without the comma. (I do actually think that one side of my arse is bigger than the other and have taken to staring at other women's arses in order to prove to myself that I am neither a freak of nature nor a victim of a lop-sided expanding-arse syndrome. The jury is currently out.)

There have been zillions (well, one or two) books recently on work-life balance.

Now I take issue with this whole thing on two fronts:

1.   If I am not living when I am at work, what exactly am I doing? Do I — unbeknown to myself — enter a non-life state for the numerous hours I am at work? Have I been missing some parallel universe experience? If so, I wish to register a complaint because I would be doing way more random naughty stuff if I could get away with it. Am I genuinely a zombie at work? Answers on a postcard.

2.   What, if anything, is ever in balance? I say this (and I apologise in advance) as a bit of a scientist. The whole business of staying in balance tends to be a very mobile thing. A series of endless, tiny giving and taking away, expanding and contracting, which, to the outside observer looks like balance. Like you on a bosu ball. A cyclist on a bike. Two kids on a see-saw. An aircraft in flight which spends more than 90% of its time off course and constantly correcting.

Hopefully you get my point.

Your life is never ever going to be completely in balance. To be so would be to imply that you have everything you want, that you are everything you need to be, that every need is fulfilled and every desire met and that the world has wrapped itself around you entirely for your benefit. And, bliss though that may sound on first reading, you would end up miserable because we were born with a need to grow.

Look at lottery winners. Few make it out intact and better for the experience, no matter how much they thought it would be positively life-enhancing. The trouble is that it takes maturity, inner wisdom and drive to handle unexpected wealth — and actually to handle any wealth at all.

Out of balance is alive. It's your muscles and intellect and psyche and heart all recognising what matters and what doesn't, and doing something about it. It's having to stretch yourself to be all you can be for the people, causes and demands you need to support.

SUTRA: Balance is not still. It's a constant movement. Don't stress, just adjust.

25

SISTERS ARE DOING IT FOR THEMSELVES

We've pretty much taken the sexual ground back, levelled the playing field. At least in the developed world.

We can ask men out, initiate sex, refuse sex, be adventurous and propose marriage — all without raising an eyebrow. We can dress as we want and do what we want.

We aren't surprised when we read of women behaving as only men used to behave.

But, sometimes, in behaving like men, we are taking on some of the less attractive male traits. And we're getting many of the same male illnesses. Heart attacks, strokes, liver disease — all rising in women as we replicate a traditionally male lifestyle — at work and in the bedroom.

So, it's time we got a few facts straight about where we're really heading as women:

- We may or may not find partners who may or may not stick around to share life's financial burdens and challenges.

- There will likely be no state pension of any substance when we get old.

- The chances of many of us building up substantial, useful pensions of our own are low.

- Some of us may make a fortune. Most of us will make a living.

- We will live long lives.

- We will, generally be healthy in old age (if we knock off the booze, fags and doughnuts).

- There will not be enough (state or private) affordable care for us in old age.

- We only have ourselves to depend upon.

- Ergo, we are fucked, possibly.

On the other hand:

- As you have read, we are better equipped than men to build up a range of work to support ourselves.

- If we start now, life could be better than ever before as we age.

- All we have to do is take responsibility for ourselves.

- Ergo, we are fucked for sure but only in a very good way.

SUTRA: Take responsibility for yourself. We are women. The future is ours for the taking.

WORKING MODELS

Work takes many forms. A job, a career, a vocation, something that you do to make a bit of cash now and again, the lifeline that supports a whole family, an interest, a passion.

Too often I hear people saying they can't find a job. I would find it hard to find a job now. But I can always find work.

An employed job, in an office, remote working for an employer, freelance, part-time, virtual, your own boss, micro jobs, at home, from overseas, on Skype, by webinar, endless combinations of any of the above... the list is long and growing.

It's all work. Some of it pays in money today and some doesn't. But the chances are it can be made to pay in some way in the future.

Your ability to recognise your talents and work out how to make them pay, is what buys you freedom. And it's never too soon — or too late — to start.

26

CELIBACY

Some people never get round to sex. Or they get round to it and then give it up. Like married people sometimes (when once you've bagged the man and the kids you're too knackered/satisfied to do what brought you together in the first place).

Whilst I have no desire to embrace celibacy, I understand that in some conditions it happens. Take nuns for instance. That's fair. They are actually doing work of the highest order, whether you believe in God or not.

Trustafarians can fall into the 'no sex' analogy too. I think it is safe to say that anyone who is gifted with enough money never to work has been handed a poisoned chalice. Unless they are equally gifted with a drive to create stuff or help the unfortunate — in other words, to make their own work — they have a tendency to slither off the rails. Even if they manage to cling on to the rails, without a purpose they are like human bonsai trees, forever stunted by a lack of challenge and the opportunity for self-fulfilment.

Then there are women who marry and give up work. Which is, of course, not giving up work at all unless you employ so many staff you spend all day at the gym, shopping and having coffee with friends. Running a home and raising kids is work in itself. These days less and less women can afford to do this — two incomes are becoming a necessity, not a luxury.

But if you do fall into this category, remember that your children will grow up and leave home; your partner may or may not stay interesting to you, interested in you, or actually stay at all.

So, if only so that you don't lose yourself in your relationship, or lose yourself altogether, find what your work could be. Just imagine if you will, living to the age of ninety, knowing and experiencing pretty much *no more* than you know now. Utterly terrifying isn't it?

Even if its a hobby, an interest or a cause — create possible work. It may just save your sanity. It will certainly make you more interesting to yourself.

SUTRA: Work is what keeps us alive and growing. Money or no money, use your work muscles.

27

SOUL MATE, SOUL WORK

Finding your soul mate is the most wonderful thing. The word 'wonderful' doesn't even touch it. We dream about it, fantasise about it, sing about it, write poetry about it. We see people who are with their soul mates and we envy them. They are the ones who will overcome any obstacle, live through any difficulty just to be together, because to do anything else would be unimaginable.

Years ago it was only a fortunate few who expected to find the work equivalent, soul work. For the rest of us, it was, "What are you going to be when you grow up?", to a lot of blank faces all round.

For some there was an answer and that answer became a reality. Doctors, vets, priests, teachers, singers, actors, artists — very often know what they are going to be because somehow that is what they ARE even before they are.

One of my clients found her soul work in medicine. She will be engaged in that for the whole of her life as there is no finite end to what she does except her own death. When she can no longer practise she will probably write and lecture about her passion.

A friend found his in photography. It is his love, his work and his means of earning a good living.

Your soul work may simply be a thread that runs through everything you do, a theme that keeps repeating itself. For me, it's teaching in some way shape or form. No matter what I do, I end up teaching, even though it is not often overtly called that.

If you find that soul work, cherish it and nurture it. Be aware that you are blessed.

Remember that not everyone finds their soul work. For those of us who don't, we need to learn to recognise when our souls *are* being nurtured and see the thread that causes that to happen.

And like great sex, when that happens it is orgasmic.

SUTRA: Look for what keeps drawing you to it. There is your soul work.

28

MISSIONARY

Now, don't get me wrong. There is nothing wrong with missionary. It's just a little, well, unimaginative. But, that said, it can be very safe and comforting and really rather lovely when done well. And for a lot of people it's all they ever really want to do. Which is fine because this is your life and you get to do what you want.

However, I have to say that it can a bit on the passive side. And if you don't break out of it now and again you stand to miss out on a lot of fun. All sorts of things keep people in missionary position — fear, embarrassment, lack of knowledge. None of these will kill you. A bit of spice is nice.

Missionary in the work sense is one long-term job of no obvious excitement or challenge — forty years with no discernible amusement in the Civil Service for instance. The end game is to stop doing it with a pension that's enough to keep you going till you die. Hopefully even enough to let you take a few more holidays. Very often people use this work as simply a way of paying the bills. *Life* is what they do outside of work. That's fine if you are truly fulfilled outside of your work and don't mind spanking a full 50% of your waking time on something that doesn't stimulate you. But it comes with some pretty major risk factors:

- You might die of boredom.

- Your job might be taken from you.

- You might not live long enough to get the pension and finally have the life you waited forty years to get.

- You might be too old, bored and knackered by then to enjoy it anyway.

- The pension might be nicked by your employer/the government/the markets (delete as necessary).

- You might miss the chance to find your other Russian dolls.

- You find towards the end of your missionary tenure that in fact you always wanted to be something else (sometimes ANYTHING else), and you find your life rather wasted and your soul corroded. Not that I want to scare you or anything...

This last point is very close to what can happen through celibacy. When you simply aren't forced to work through necessity or desire, and somehow potter a few decades away before waking up one morning and realising that you came here to do rather more than you have achieved.

At which point any number of things can happen — you make huge dramatic changes in your personality, you buy a motorbike and leathers and make a complete tit of yourself, you leave your spouse, career, children and go off to find yourself, you lose yourself at the bottom of a bottle of whatever you can get your hands on...

I could go on. You can tell that I am not wildly in favour of missionary work. Mainly because they are often jobs where you abdicate control for far too long and fail to notice the new things that are often hiding in plain sight.

Nothing stays the same, so if you want to stay in your missionary work, be an agent for change at your workplace. Go on, shake things up a bit.

Or if you are one of those people who works as a credit clerk by day but a burlesque dancer by night, good on you.

SUTRA: If your work has no passion in it, find it somewhere. In work or out, find what floats your boat.

29

SERIAL MONOGAMY

Some people are slow burners. They like to get deeply into relationships, until they get back out of them again. Sometimes it's of their choosing — new times, new partner — or sometimes they get left behind when someone else moves on. But the underlying thing is that they like to get in deep and stay there for a pretty long time.

It can be a bit traumatic if and when it ends. For serial monogamists, they form wider connections within their relationships and it can be tough to take those apart and start again.

They usually think pretty deeply about moving on — after all, a lot has been invested already. Not just time but experience and money.

Mark is a barrister. He was a doctor and changed careers in his forties, taking silk in his late fifties.

Evelyn was a vet. Her entire family was horrified when, after years in training and more than a decade in practice, she retrained as a lawyer. Two people going in almost identical but opposite directions.

This is where we are so much more fortunate than previous generations. Even fifty years ago it would have been unheard of to switch professional horses late in life. But of course, late in life now is later still. It wouldn't be impossible for someone now to decide in their sixties to set off on a new path. The universal derision meted out when a politician recently suggested that retirees go to university was unfair. He didn't say it well but, just as our sex life isn't over in our sixties, neither is our learning or working life.

Even better is when young people recognise early that the path they have chosen is wrong for them and make a change quickly. James studied Medical Biology but soon realised he wasn't cut out for a life in a laboratory. He retrained as a lawyer and is now happily at work. It wasn't easy and he had to be persistent but better a few tough years now than decades stuck in something you don't like.

We don't know what anything will be like until we do it. And if we find we don't like it, we owe it to ourselves to do something about it.

Never be afraid to make a change. Regret is always retrospective, when it is too late to do anything about it.

SUTRA: You are not your job title. It's only the thing you are doing just now.

30

THE FLIRT

Lord knows, flirting is fun. In fact, it can be such huge fun that you never quite move beyond it. And that's not such a bad thing, I think.

It seems to me that if you are young and looking at decades of work and a long life then maybe we need to be shaping life differently. Why follow the pattern of choosing a job or career, starting it at 20 or so and keeping going relentlessly just to fit into what society expects?

Why save for old age when what you can save is a pittance anyway? (Word of caution — this is not as flippant as it sounds. Like anything else in life, freedom comes with responsibilities. See below.)

If nothing particularly grabs you, but you're keen, bright, willing and energetic, why not just do whatever you can get and dip in and out of work as it suits you?

Take a year out and travel when you're forty? Why not?

Take your 'retirement' when you're 35 and then go back to work? Do it!

Maybe you just love to do something that is pretty all-consuming. You love to surf, for instance. So, you do whatever work you can get to support you doing that. You keep your needs pretty basic and don't need to earn much. That's fine, if temperamentally you're up for it.

The only requirements for this kind of work life are:

• Natural optimism — you can't do this if you are constantly panicked about where the next pay cheque is coming from.

• Ability to manage money and a budget.

- Ability to learn fast and cross fertilise your knowledge — you're going to self-educate so you need to pay attention.

- Ability to spot opportunity and sell yourself in.

- Being a good reader — stay on top of trends so you can get in there quick.

- A relaxed attitude to assets — you'll likely never buy a house but then again, neither will a lot of people.

- A mature attitude to work — you might feel foot loose and fancy free, and you are, but you've got to act dedicated to whatever you're doing. In other words, fake it, for everyone's benefit.

This style works particularly well if the only exam you've ever passed is a smear test. No one said that school was the only place to learn, after all...

SUTRA: It's your life. Do it the way you want. But take responsibility.

31

SEX GURU

Sexual therapy is on the up and up apparently. Women are flocking to a chap in London for hands-on sexual awakening. They wouldn't call it that in Soho.

He gets his clients by word of mouth. And the odd article in the national press hasn't harmed.

There's a lot to be said for getting a name for yourself.

Celebrity is everywhere. Reality TV has a lot to answer for — people all over the place with bugger-all talent and no work ethic wanting to become overnight successes.

But, now that anyone can become anything, pretty much, what if you ACTUALLY had something useful and valuable to say? What if you knew things that could help people make money, be healthier, be more knowledgeable, be happier?

If you have something worth spreading, it's never been easier to spread it. Blogging, tweeting (I know, I know, but it all works in one way or another), offering to share your wisdom for free for a while — to build your platform.

Get out there. Teaching, talking, demonstrating that you're an expert. Get some results for people and then spread the news.

Write a book, maybe?

Do videos on YouTube. That's how Khan Academy got started — then Bill Gates stumbled across it and invested.

Build the brand that is you.

Just one thing to bear in mind — unlike overnight celebrity, chances are you've taken decades learning what you know, or experienced something very profound that will help others. This is not the place to be a charlatan. Make sure that you really *do* make a difference.

Because once your name is out there, you can't get it back.

SUTRA: Get great at something then help others to get great.

32

MULTIPLE ORGASMS

Now here's the thing. Sexually I think this is a bit of a myth for most people. Which doesn't mean it's not worth striving and hoping for. For most women just one would be enough, especially if they didn't have to do it themselves. But at least in theory, it's a possibility for everyone.

At work it's rather like having each of your Russian dolls out there all at the same time. Now you might only have one or two or you might have several. Not all of them need to be earning you money at any one time. But the more pleasure you get in one area, the more pleasure you tend to find elsewhere. Pleasure has a wonderful way of making us see the world differently.

Like the early days of falling in love, when suddenly the slog to work is full of happy fellow travellers instead of smelly arm-pitted grunts, and the girl at Pret who normally pisses you off suddenly seems charmingly effusive instead of just fucking annoying and SHOUTY.

Getting as much pleasure as possible is a GOOD THING.

Being multiply orgasmic usually means people think you are doing too much and should focus on one thing. Sod that. Multiple orgasms require a lot of stroking, as in you are a 'plumber/teacher/artist'. If you can pull off stroking — multiple work/jobs simultaneously — to a high enough level, you will probably be having the most fun of anyone you know, getting your pleasure right, left and centre.

An example of this (and there aren't many at a very high level yet, we're just getting into the swing of this) is Anna, who is an actress, a photographer, a dance teacher, an audio book narrator, an illustrator, a proof-reader and the curator of a small art collection. All paid. In her spare time she runs the local community group, reads to old people in their homes and does ballet herself. She's seventy-one.

Anna is an example of extending her interests into paid work that, money or no money, means she is also never bored or boring. The trick is to keep trying out new things.

And if, no matter how hard you try, you just can't climax with one, dump it. If it pays the bills, work on how to dump it ASAP or modify it to be more fun. Plan your escape, write your leaving speech — but preferably not on your work PC unless you plan to lose control of the timing, and we all know timing is everything when it comes to orgasms.

SUTRA: In the case of work orgasms, there is no such thing as too much of a good thing.

33

MADAME

Now this is my all time favourite.

This is what more and more women are doing. They are setting up shop for themselves. Not red lights in windows in Shepherd Market, or shady bungalows in Woking.

But in bedrooms and kitchens and borrowed offices and boardrooms all over the world.

In the US there has been a 45% increase in businesses started by women since 1997. The UK is not far behind. Worldwide, female entrepreneurs are producing much of the world's GDP — but no one is paying any attention.

The average age of first-time entrepreneurs is rising, not falling.

Being a Madame can range from being a sole trader (you), to the CEO of your own multi- million pound business (and that can still be just you. Take Delia Smith, no slouch when it comes to making dough).

Or Martha Lane-Fox of LastMinute.com.

Or Michelle Mone of Ultimo bras.

Or Dessi Bell of Zaggora.

The list is long and getting longer with numerous unnoticed success stories. Just like the original Madames, beavering (sorry, couldn't stop myself) away in the shadows, our new Madames are quietly setting up businesses and designing their own lives.

And we do it differently. We start with less capital then men. We are more likely to leave a job to start a business than a man. We take on less debt than men.

We grow more slowly. But we fail less often and less quickly.

We employ more women. Cool, huh? That's mainly because we break away from the presentee-ism of male-dominated corporates.

And, no, I don't subscribe to the Marissa Mayer (CEO of Yahoo) theory of work. Building a nursery next door to your office and then banning remote working for your staff is an act of blatant hypocrisy and selfishness, and a demonstration of total lack of trust in your people.

You can be a part-time Madame until you get into your stride. It is, once you get used to it, perfect freedom.

And it has never been easier to do it.

SUTRA: Doing it for yourself is always a good thing.

34

CYBER SEX

Sexting. Exchanging sexy pictures. Phone sex. Internet porn. All cyber sex.

The only thing missing in cyber sex is a real person to touch. Cyber sex still fires up excitement, creates physical and chemical changes and leads to orgasm. In other words, it does the job, virtually.

Now, some work really needs real people in a room together, talking to each other, much of the time.

Most businesses need their people to bounce off each other now and again, to get ideas, to keep in touch with what is going on and solve problems.

Some kinds of work can only be done in one particular place — like a hospital or school.

But mainly we go to an office because that's what we're used to doing. We also get asked to go to offices because people (e.g. Marissa Mayer again) do not believe that we can be trusted to get together when we need to and to work alone when it is appropriate.

In other words we do not behave, nor are we treated like, grown-ups.

It is like marrying someone and then never being allowed to be apart. Christ, frequent separation from each other is often the only thing that keeps people together.

So, following on from Madame, either as a lone wolf or part of a pack, make sure you have all your sex toys (see later) in working order and then add in as much cyber sex as you can. You can be in business, or working for a business, from anywhere, at anytime. I work with businesses in Geneva, France, Australia, the US and Singapore. Two of those businesses do not have two people on the same continent. There are no barriers any more because technology has broken them down.

As an example, here is what I use (and remember, I am no guru, this lot is required stuff if you are in business or working remotely pretty much, and almost all free or nearly free):

- Dropbox.com for storing and sharing files.

- Capsulecrm.com or any other CRM system for CRM and prospect tracking.

- Basecamp for project sharing.

- Mailchimp for bulk mailing.

- Wordpress for blogging and website.

- Powwownow for conference calling.

- Wetransfer.com for sending REALLY big files.

- Bitly.com for shortening URLs for tweeting.

- Prezi.com for easier than PowerPoint presentations.

- Xero or Freeagent accounts package (online and links into Capsule).

- Join.me for free screen sharing,

- Go To Meeting/Go to Webinar (both paid) if you run group meetings or webinars.

- Google+ for informal 'hangouts' of up to 9 people.

- Answer.com/JAM for phone answering.

- E-Draw max for creating process flowcharts.

- SmartSheet for creating timeline Gant Charts.

- Toodledo for to-do lists (with GTD (Getting Things Done) app on my phone).

- eWallet for password storage.

- Hootsuite for social media monitoring and updates.

- Mindjet MindManager for mind maps.

- Cloud Contacts for processing scanned business cards.

- Receipt Bank for processing expenses receipts.

- My Virtual Assistant, Lesley, for absolutely everything else. (She's real, by the way.)

SUTRA: Work does not mean a job or a location. Work is where you are.

GET YOUR COAT, YOU'VE PULLED

It's all very well there being numerous different ways of working but how do you find them? If you're stuck at home, or in an office job or ploughing through a career you no longer love, how on earth do you know where to go next?

Just as sex doesn't have to be in bed or for that matter always with the same person, work doesn't have to be in an office or doing the same thing.

The secret is to make a point of noticing work — what it is and where it is — a part of what you do.

It is, of course, very like how you find a man, should you want one. You get about a bit...

35

A BIT ON THE SIDE

God, I love a bit on the side.

Some of my bits on the side have been the highlights of my life. Frankly, life has been made a damn sight more fun by my endless tendency to flirt with various little peccadilloes. Some not so little and some considerably more than flirting. One or two have become permanent features and therefore moved from the sidelines into the main event.

Like writing. Many years ago, I wrote a novel for my own entertainment. It was utterly shit but doing it at all taught me that I could get out 3,000 words a day, typed by my own fair hands — well about four fingers. My typing is no better today. But my writing has come along. In the twenty years since I tapped out that novel, I've made money writing sales letters, articles, case studies, and website content.

How do you fit a bit on the side into your already busy life? How do you get clandestine moments of illicit writing, painting, reading, studying, moon-lighting, plotting and planning into an already packed schedule?

First of all, you choose something that turns you on. Even just a little. A little frisson of curiosity, a tiny buzz of 'what if?'. Just enough of an interest to keep you going for a bit until you work out how you really feel about it.

We all get the same number of hours in the day. And we all get to choose what we do with them. The hour you spend each week — even better, the half hour you spend most days — trying something new, is more valuable than all the hours spent watching crap TV or sitting on Facebook.

Get up earlier, go to bed later. If you want it enough you'll get up at 5am happily. Trust me, one of my bits on the side often requires a 5am start and is worth every single second of it.

Get someone else to cook dinner. Get a take away. Stay out after work — once you get home it's hard to get back out again. Squeeze your squeeze into lunchtimes.

It might only be a fling, it might become an affair or you may fall in love. Whatever, it will be one more thing you know about yourself. And your brain will have changed because you've used a new bit of it.

Take Greg, for instance. A real technologist who made a fair chunk of money from his last job. And a cricket freak. He started making bespoke gear for cricket clubs and is now running a proper little business.

SUTRA: Make a deliberate and consistent effort to expand your repertoire.

36

FOREPLAY

Oh my word, the damage that porn has done. Everyone seems so keen to get straight down to business now. Apparently we can all get straight to fireworks without so much as a spark being lit. All preliminaries seem to have been forgotten. And yet, and yet...

Foreplay is one of the best bits. Sometimes it is THE best bit. (All right, sometimes it's the ONLY good bit...) Finding out new things, feeling new feelings. Being open to possibilities. No rushing, just gentle and absorbing exploration.

That's how we learn about each other.

And it's the same with new work of any description. Even work that isn't work to start with. Work that is just stuff, something you do. A hobby, an interest, a fetish...

And when you've got a bit on the side, it's more important than ever. You're in uncharted territory. Things are unfamiliar. You know what you're used to so, even though it can be exciting, it's also scary. We scare fast (remember those amygdala?).

And chances are you'll be doing it in a different place, without the comfort of familiar people and locations.

Take Annabelle. She liked to go to shows and plays. She's a shipping lawyer in her day job and thought of herself as practical and forensic and the opposite of creative. But when she saw a local theatre struggling to cope she pitched in, simply because she loved going there and didn't want it to close. Mind you, she needed that passion to get her rocking up evening after evening, tired and stressed from cargoes sunk and contracts lost or broken. But it wasn't work to her, of course. It was recreation.

Within two years (see, she stuck at it...) she was collaborating on scripts, sitting in on rehearsals, organising auditions. Now, she can see where she will go in due course, when all her ships have sailed.

SUTRA: With foreplay, do it for longer than you thought. It will pay off.

37

SPEED DATING

I've done this. More than once. Twice in fact, the second time only to prove to myself that I would rather gnaw my own arm off than do it again. (By the way, this was more than twenty years ago, just in case you were worrying.)

However, second time round I took a new approach. On the principle that I was not expecting to find Mr Passable, far less Mr Right, I was relaxed and actually prepared to have some fun. I did. I am not entirely sure the guys I sat opposite enjoyed it quite so much but there we are.

So, if you can't get a bit on the side, if nothing catches your eye, you really want to be playing the numbers game.

You see, you might not know it but you're stuck. You know what you know. And that's all that you know. You've also forgotten much of the stuff that used to float your boat. Now you're a 'grown up', you think you're sorted.

Nope.

You are not sorted. You have a 'list'. You're stale, frozen, and predictable. You buy coffee in the same coffee shop. You wear 10% of your wardrobe. Your hair has been the same for the last five years. You probably even have very much the same conversations with the same few friends. You could, if pushed, replace yourself with a pre-recording.

Don't be offended. I'm sure you are lovely and vibrant and amazing. In fact, I know it. And no matter how glittering you are on the surface, unless you purposefully make yourself try new things, learn new skills, do some stuff that you might just truly hate just so you can say you've tried, your blood will thicken and your brain cells will stop talking to each other.

Dammit. Put yourself about a bit. Pitch in with anything new you can find; try everything; join in a different group at work; do a new sport; offer help where you see a need. You're not made of stone.

SUTRA: Be putty. But in your own hands.

38

FRIENDS WITH BENEFITS

FWBs are great. None of the hassle, all of the fun. Remarkably risk free in fact.

With a FWB, you get the chance to scratch an itch and, once scratched, you stay mates. The secret to successful FWBs is that you both get something out of it and neither of you has any hidden agenda. There is nothing more damaging to a friendship than a one-sided FWB relationship, when one of you is secretly harbouring hopes that it will turn into 'something more'.

FWBs can only be done by grown-ups.

At work, I like to think of it as advanced lubrication.

Let me explain.

I have a friend, Nick. He is in an entirely different industry to anything I have even been in. He doesn't get my world and his is as alien to me an actual alien.

But, to us, business is just business. Whether it's managing a band (Nick), building a technology business, making babies (me, but not personally) or trading oil, there are basics that apply. The trick is to know what the fundamentals are for that industry. The rest you can pick up as you go along.

Over time Nick and I have spent a lot of time drinking wine and talking about life, the universe and each others' work. The fact that work is so much of all of our lives means that no personal conversation can last long without work popping up somewhere.

But this is not just any old (alcoholic) lubrication.

We have discovered that we get along really well, have similar values and sense of humour (it helps). We both also want to keep building out more work opportunities and spot random connections.

We don't want to be in business bed with each other. But we do know that we can find work by snuggling up together.

So, we work actively on it. We meet regularly and we invite each other into meetings with relevant colleagues, on the off-chance that something might arise. We get our two groups of friends and associates together, and these are people who would never in a million years have met each other normally, to see what happens. And we happen to have a ball whilst we do it.

The result? The whole is greater than the sum of the parts.

SUTRA: Put together a group of mutually interested people and leverage off each other.

39

HAND JOB

Sometimes, we all need a little helping hand. Sometimes it's nicer when someone else does something for us. And sometimes it's good to do something for someone else. To lend a hand, to give pleasure, and relief...

The one thing we can say for sure is that there is no shortage of people needing a hand for all sorts of things.

You'll have worked out by now that I believe in giving first and getting later. It works, as well as feeling good.

If you want to learn more about an area of work, or to show what you can do, offer to do it for nothing for a bit.

Need is rarely visible. If it is, you can simply pounce on it and pitch in to help. But some people or businesses don't even know that they need you, until you suggest what you might be able to do for them.

If you can get specific, it's easier. Once you can define the experience you want to have, you can root it out. We all know that until we try something we don't really know what it is like. We also know that we have to give it time, to get over the unfamiliarity of it, so that we can assess it properly. Hand jobs rock for this.

I know we are shackled by bloody Health and Safety, Employment Regulations, Criminal Record checking (and, yes, I know we need to protect the young, old and vulnerable but is the world really full of so many evil people?) — BUT there are still endless places you can go to offer unpaid help.

If you want to see how a design studio works, or a ship broker, or a personal shopper (these last three are all things I was asked about recently) — find people who do whatever it is that interests you and offer to carry their bags, fetch their lunch, do their admin, make their appointments, do their grunt work.

Seriously, if you are going to get anywhere you need to get your balls out (ladies, you DO have balls. In your head). Ask people. Take risks.

And this is not just advice for young people, although it is precisely what they should be doing all the time. It might not be what they had in mind but internships are just another way of testing the waters to see what you're good at and showcasing yourself. In the end, we're likely all going to end up doing it at some time.

(And, if you want to do your soul some good, now and again just do something for someone for no other reason than that they need it. It's karmic money in the bank.)

SUTRA: Buy experience by giving yourself away free.

VOYEUR

Now it doesn't matter if you want to admit it or not, but there is an endless fascination in watching other people having sex. Whether the fascination is mild shyness, excruciating embarrassment, scandalised horror, or a total turn on, it's hard to drag our eyes away.

And sometimes you find yourself thinking: "How do they do that?"

Often it's: "Why do they do that?"

It's a way to get more involved without any risk of exposure ourselves. A sort of vicarious pleasure.

That's what being a voyeur at work is for too. Getting yourself engaged, immersed in what someone else does, finding out how they do it, what makes them tick, what fascinates them, what is good, bad and indifferent about what they do.

The more bonkers the better. It's the bonkers stuff that catches your eye and its from bonkers stuff that you get new ideas.

The easiest way to spot a potential idea is when you find yourself asking yourself: "Why does no one do/make that?" or "Why on earth do they do it that way?"

If you spot something you would like, or see something being done badly, chances are others would too. And once you spot a gap, you can consider how you might plug it.

Because new industries are popping up all the time and new work is popping up with them, often as a by-product. They are there just waiting for someone to spot the need.

And a new world creates opportunity, with people squeezing the most out of margins and time. Here are a few of the bonkers and brilliant ideas that are fulfilling a need and making people some cash:

- There are people who write blogs for businesses and run their twitter feeds.

- Mobile bike repair businesses are popping up all over as more and more people cycle to work.

- Hair salons that do a fifteen-minute blow dry for £15. Perfect for busy, working women.

- If you can be a zombie — the London Dungeon will audition you.

- Golf ball divers — a good one can find one million balls a year. That will earn you about £100k pa.

All you need is to keep looking around with a sense of curiosity. You can and will uncover a need somewhere that you can look to fill. If not you, who?

SUTRA: Look for the unusual. Find a gap and work out how it might be filled.

DOMINATRIX

A LOT of men like bossy women. Many will pay for it.

Although it's work, I'm not suggesting you go in that direction, but you can always bear it in mind...

Look, we all know that women can be bossy. The world runs on bossy women — even the clandestine ones who hide their strength.

One of my friends calls me a kitten with a whip. I kind of like that. In reality, I guess being a dominatrix is what got me to where I am now.

A dominatrix is the voyeur in action. It's you taking a risk that you can really impact on a business or a situation — but instead of causing pain, you're going to take it away.

It starts with being a voyeur and then gives you the opportunity to become a dominatrix by implementing what you see is needed.

You've got to be tough and confident — even when you don't quite know what you're walking in to. That's OK, you can learn on the job. It's a great route for anyone who has pulled off big jobs in the past and recognises that most problems are simple if you just break them down.

And being a dominatrix is the one time to get paid — often modestly until you get a reputation — as you practise. Because you offer to improve or fix something that is damaging a business and you negotiate to get paid WHEN IT WORKS. You're sharing the risk with them. If you fail to deliver what they need, you don't get paid.

This is like an apprenticeship. Before you can turn it into proper paying work you have to prove to yourself that you can pull off the results. Once you have you can then get some recommendations or referrals, refine your skills, and practically name your salary. Everyone needs a feisty fixer in their lives.

SUTRA: Trouble shoot. And crack the whip.

42

SEX TOYS

It's always been boys' toys, hasn't it? Right up until the rabbit (not the fluffy one) and Ann Summers on a High Street near you. Now our toys put our pleasure into our own hands.

But of course, the toys we really need to master don't stay in the bedroom.

I have been surprised — no, that's way too much of an understatement — I have been STAGGERED by how many women are technophobes.

Sure, they can pout for a selfie and stick it on Instagram. They can stream their photos onto flickr and download music from Spotify or Deezr. Facebook is permanently open on their iPhones or androids and they can send party invites to 300 best friends while shopping in TopShop.

But ask them to use Word, Excel or PowerPoint with any degree of skill and they're sunk.

At the other end of the age range, I have sat opposite a fifty-year-old whilst she struggled to save a file in Word on a PC.

I hear too many women telling me with a wry shrug that they haven't got to grips with this or that technology.

To which I want to scream: GET A GRIP!

Now, I am excruciatingly aware that my daughter will be reading this and howling with laughter. I am the woman who still can't change my profile picture on Facebook. My use of my iPad is pathetic and I reckon I use about 10% of the functions on my iPhone.

I am, however, fit for purpose for my working life.

I can create, store, work with and send documents in all the usual formats. I can set up and run conference calls and webinars. I can change and manage my own website. (For more on this see Cyber Sex.) Dammit, I am even fully loaded on how to use LinkedIn.

It is not charming to be technologically incompetent in a technological world. It is suicide.

Man up to technology.

SUTRA: Oil your toys and hone your skills.

DON'T LIE ON THE WET PATCH

It's a fact that, no matter how brave, strong and capable we are, even the best of us can occasionally find work less than wonderful.

A sense of humour helps, of course. Sometimes you need just a bit more than that though.

43

BASTARDS

The saying goes that 'All men are...'

No, they're not. But those that are do take some handling.

I once worked with an insufferable bully. Although I was not reporting directly to him, he could and did make my life a misery. And I took way too long to realise what was happening because bullies are usually cunning. Note I don't say clever because that's not a given. But because they are operating from a need for superiority (therefore some sort of issue in themselves), they are way ahead of everyone in manipulation.

Bastards are not always bullies and bullies are not always men (see Bitches). But they usually are because it comes with the territory.

Sometimes they are just plain bad-tempered. Sometimes they shout and hurl abuse.

Sometimes they change what they want just to confuse and upset you.

They are all, to a man, beneath contempt.

There is only one starting place for dealing with bastards.

You have to know that you can and will walk if you have to. Simple.

If you know you can leave and you plan for how that might happen, you can afford to fight back because you have nothing to lose.

I'm not going to pretend it's easy. It's not. But that's why it matters that you keep open-minded about your ability to find work. You buy yourself the chance to stand up for yourself without being broken by fear of what will happen to you.

The first time to answer back is the first time he is mean to you. And you have to stay consistent and calm. Keep notes, record dates, refute errors and complaints formally and logically.

Personally, that's why I like being my own boss. And it's a good reason to keep that as an option.

Never let anyone dictate how you feel. And DO NOT allow yourself to damage your life.

Nothing is ever that important. Nothing.

SUTRA: Deal with bullies day one and always have an escape plan.

BITCHES

Oh my dears, I fear I will be dragged out onto the streets and stoned for this. By women.

In my experience there is very little sodding sisterhood. Sure, I have met many helpful and supportive women, just as I have met many helpful and supportive men. I have also met women and men who are frankly downright obstructive and jealous about offering any form of help.

People are just people.

The notion that women will universally rally around each other is utter bollocks.

An unhelpful woman rarely stops at just being unhelpful. She turns into a bitch of the highest order.

And a bitch will make your life a misery more than any man can at work. Because she knows how to push your buttons, she can be a bit more devious. (I know, it's a generalisation but it's true. Women are devious. There, I said it.) Or they will come across all sweetness and light and block you at every turn.

We're still not used to a level playing field, so some women get ahead and pull the ladder up after themselves.

Some form alliances and tribes, just like at school when the nasty girls picked on the soft ones.

Some sacrifice everything for work and then can't tolerate anyone else who tries to do it differently. (See Yahoo.)

Some think they have to be tougher than tough to get on, so they do longer hours than any man and expect other women to do the same.

It's not easy, I know.

How to deal with it?

Same as bastards.

Tackle it head on from day one in precisely the same way you would deal with a man.

But in both cases, sometimes it's easier and more effective to simply choose differently. Decide what works for you and then find a place where how you like to work and be treated (and treat others) works for everyone else too. You can't stomp into a culture and change it by force unless you are prepared to be de-railed and exhausted by the fight. Choose the right culture for you. It's easier that way.

(And for those of you who want to fight for change, fine. But beware of a blanket faith in the power of women to humanise the workplace. Some of us will. Some won't. And some of what will happen will not cover us with glory. You have been warned.)

SUTRA: You may be a great woman. But just focus on being a good human first.

45

KISSING FROGS

I nearly just put this into Bastards. But then I thought, nope, frogs are special. They deserve a place of their own.

In the process of finding a lover, or a job, or work, you will have to take people at face value.

You know when you meet a guy and he shows potential. Just potential, mind. Not obviously 'the one' or even just hot as hell, but neither is he obviously and completely wrong.

Now, I assume that you have standards to a certain level about what face value means. So at least day one, he looks like a possibility, no obvious tics, odours, habits, conditions etc. that might set off the alarm bells.

So far, so good.

Here is the difference between a frog and a bastard (or a bitch).

A frog does not know he is a frog. Whilst the behaviours he demonstrates in due course obviously rule him well out of the Prince category, he is just himself.

That could mean he's a liar, mean, smelly, devoted to his mother, obsessed by snakes or rottweilers. It's irrelevant. He is what he is. And that happens to be NOT for us. And the only way to find out is to take time, be observant and if possible, find out as much as you can from whoever you can. So if his ex took out a restraining order on him, he might not be the one for you.

I once set up a business with what appeared to be a very charming, capable man. A very short while into our venture it became apparent that he had the morals of an alley cat in business terms. It cost me thousands of pounds to get out of the business and wasted a year of my time.

My fault. I could have found it out if I had really asked around, but he was so charming...

It took me a long time to accept that it was my fault for not documenting every single detail of our venture, for not doing rigorous due diligence on him. But trust is NOT a given at the start of any relationship or venture. Dig deep until you can evidence to yourself that what you see is what you want.

For me, it was an expensive and bruising lesson. But I now know how to boil the bloody frogs before they poison me.

SUTRA: Trust comes from knowledge. Make yourself an expert on possible partners of any kind.

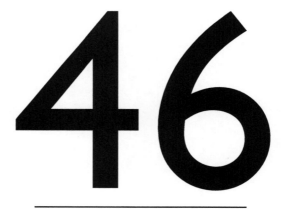

SEX ADDICTS

Guilty as charged, M'Lud.

I am addicted to all sorts of things but especially to work.

And like all addictions, it is an altered state of being. You are incapable of rational thought.

Every now and again I have to smack myself around the face with a wet fish and remind myself that:

- I am not indispensable to any client.

- I am not going to end up sleeping under London Bridge.

- I have all sorts of opportunities and can probably make more money with less effort if I just STOP sometimes.

- Kids, grandchildren, lovers, friends, exercise, recreation and even the odd holiday are GOOD for me. WAY better than endless hours working.

If you become an addict, slap yourself. Or task someone else with the job of doing it to you.

I have worked in places and with people for whom I have sacrificed my entire personal life. I have been repeatedly told by them how invaluable I am to the business. I have then been shafted. Work is wonderful — but there are other things you could and should be doing to enrich your life. So, take some days off and do them. You have a long time to work. There's no rush. Trust me.

SUTRA: Work should enhance your life, not consume it.

47

LIMP DICKS

Contrary to what this might seem, limp dicks are not exclusively male. Admittedly you may have to call them limp dildos but women can display this trait as well as men.

First things first, do not be a limp dick.

Don't be wet with a limp handshake, physically downtrodden, always putting yourself down in that 'little me' way that limp dicks do. False modesty, self-effacement taken to extremes, holding back in order to be 'coaxed' into something — it's all very icky I'm afraid.

Limp dicks are victims.

If you find yourself in the company of one, get the hell out of there.

If you work for one, it's like being led into war by a scaredy cat.

I've worked on Management Boards with limp dicks. Prior to the meeting we might have met and agreed what needed to be raised as a challenge or concern to the Chairman. I would be the appointed spokesperson. As I started to speak all heads dropped whilst they scribbled innocuously, hiding from view.

It was like marching towards the enemy and looking back only to find your troops were running for cover.

Any organisation like that is a nightmare to work in.

Limp is not good. Rigid is.

SUTRA: Work with people who know what they stand for and who will stand up for it.

48

THE 7 YEAR ITCH

Oh God, most of us have been there, or will get there. It's sort of a rite of passage.

I know a guy who is gobsmackingly gorgeous in every way. Handsome, hot body, elegant, fit... you get the idea. He is successful, intelligent, a great and generous provider, loyal, a fabulous father. I could go on but I won't as I may dribble a bit.

His wife loves him, for sure. But she takes him for granted a bit. And I dare say the same is happening in reverse. And whilst it is not likely to have repercussions right now, if it goes on it might.

We all do it in one way or another. Familiarity breeds contempt, sadly.

Now if you have a soul mate (person or work), you will not be immune to The Itch. We often end up with predictable days, weeks, even months. The Armed Forces tackle that by moving people every couple of years — not just geographically but new roles and challenges.

Nothing stays the same — not people, not jobs, not the environment.

As we know, when we're not growing, we start shrinking. We're like sharks. We have to keep moving to stay alive.

Before you chuck it all in, make sure that you've made an effort to see what is really happening. We become complacent, we think we know what is going on when in reality we don't. We can only ever see a very small part of the bigger picture.

Look for what has changed. Think of the challenges you and your work/company/business are facing today and consider how to solve them or anticipate future issues. Introduce excitement. Ask what you can do.

Make sure that you keep looking for the new and interesting in what you do. So the man you married is not the same man, you are not the same woman, your job and your work and your business and your customers and the environment are not the same either.

When you stop to think about it, that's pretty exciting really.

SUTRA: Just like your computer, you need to refresh now and again.

PREMATURE EJACULATION

Well, the unfortunate side effect of the 7 year itch is often premature ejaculation.

So what usually has to happen to stop premature ejaculation? Thinking.

Thinking about something else; pretty much anything else, and the more mundane the better.

Bus routes, football, steam-engines (oh, maybe not...)

The point is that concentrating on what is happening at that moment is not helpful. You need a wider picture.

So, whilst I am always in favour of finding new work, work can be made new. Quitting too soon is not good. (Quitting too late is damaging, mind you. It's a fine balance, just like in sex.)

We get stale, we get familiar, we accept the norms. We tell ourselves that nothing can change because nothing ever has.

But if everyone gives up, how can it change? And if it has to start somewhere, why not with you?

In your work, there's stuff you have never tackled, ideas you have never shared, conversations you have never had.

You don't have to go at it like a bull in a china shop. You can do little things to ease change into the system and past the doubters and critics.

And here is *Kaizen* again — continuous small improvement (which also slips past their amygdala so it gets embedded before anyone notices. Sneaky, huh?)

Why not be a catalyst for change INSIDE where you are?

SUTRA: If you want change, start with you.

50

50 WAYS TO LEAVE YOUR LOVER

It's one of those tricky things. Do you go for the brutal, fast exit or a gentle slow slide out with hints and innuendo?

I'm kind of all for the brutal exit but of course, as we all know, that has usually been preceded by weeks, if not months of agonising, planning, changing your mind, fears, often guilt and sadness, sometimes bitterness.

There is no easy way to say goodbye. Unless of course you are choosing to move on to new and exciting things.

Which is why I always try to make any exit elegant and positive.

If you think about lubrication, you will have worked out that everyone you ever have known is part of your network. You simply have no idea when you will bump in to or need the endorsement of someone from your past.

Make it your policy to part well from everyone. Interestingly, I have never fallen out with anyone in business except the one tosser I mentioned earlier.

At regular intervals I am asked about him but I refuse to talk negatively about him. Instead, I say I would not personally choose to work with him again. I could have passed him tons of business. I don't and won't and that speaks volumes to people who know me.

Even if you have to take issue when you leave, do it professionally and calmly. Be memorable not for your complaint but for your grace in handling it. Do not bad mouth people, do not be greedy and do not pollute remaining staff, clients or suppliers.

It might feel good to make a point and win a short-term battle but it's much better to win the war.

SUTRA: The manner of your leaving says way more about you than you might realise. Make it a good one.

51

EJACULATION

Not *that* kind of ejaculation. The hurtful kind. The kind where you're ejected from their lives. Oh God, it smarts. It's happened to us all, I guess. Well, maybe not all but most of us. No, it really has happened to us all.

It's that awful moment when you question everything about yourself.

When you can't live without him/her (even though you were a tiny bit ambivalent the day before the 'Declaration of Independence').

When you cry yourself to sleep.

When you just know in your gut you will NEVER find anyone like them. Sob.

STOP.

You will. Better, even.

When it's not right, it's not right, period. I sometimes meet people who have been made redundant several times. And they ask: Is it me? Why was I chosen?

And I don't have a clue. It might be them. They might be lazy. Or difficult to get along with. Or useless. Or serial settlers who have mentally resigned but stayed in post. I don't know.

But they probably do know the answer, if they're prepared to be honest with themselves.

Being sacked is your best (if most painful) opportunity to work out what you are like. What impact you have on people. If it's not your first time and you see a pattern, it is telling you something.

I am, admittedly, from the school of telling the brutal truth, but I apply that to myself too. When something happens and I ask for other people's opinion on it, I want them to tell me the truth. Because I don't want to be here again, experiencing this pain.

It's called being a grown up. I recommend it.

And if you happen to be in the position to make someone redundant or sack them, remember that *how* you do it will have a huge impact on them. Your job is to give them as much honesty as you can *without* taking them apart. Ideally, let them leave able to feel they can do better in the future.

SUTRA: Everyone gets rejected sometime. Learn and move on.

52

BLOODY HORMONES

Right girls, I am going to say something that I would have KILLED someone for saying twenty years ago, when my hormones had a tighter grip on my reactions.

You need to be aware of your bloody hormones. Now I am not excusing men from hormone-induced bad behaviour, no sirreee. But that's their problem.

We have to deal with ours.

Before I was thirty I had the usual monthly ups and downs. Then I had a hysterectomy, which resulted in a wide range of hormones whizzing about, which required HRT, testosterone, all sorts of shit to try and balance me out. Between thirty and fifty my head was alternately firing on all cylinders and wanting to fire a machine gun at anyone who crossed me. I could, possibly, definitely, be a bit of a bloody nightmare.

Ladies, there is NO POINT pretending that this does not happen.

We think we are being rational when frankly we are being NUTTERS.

I exclude no one from this.

You have to be aware of and manage your hormones and your behaviour. If you know you are about to go off piste in the logic stakes, change what you are doing. Distract yourself from the madness of the moment. Bite your tongue rather than blurt out what comes into your head. Modify your behaviour. Take more time to make decisions.

Pre-menstrual honesty (not unlike my whisky honesty) is easy to dish out but not always so well received. But, you have to pre-plan this because once the hormones kick in, you're fucked.

I also apply this to crying at work. If you've lost a relative or been diagnosed with cancer, sob away and I will be there for you. But crying at work about work stuff? No way. And I take this stance because if a man cried in front of me at work for anything other than the previous two reasons, I would not be impressed. So what makes a woman different?

I recognise that this is also stoning-type rhetoric. I make no apologies for it.

SUTRA: You are a biological woman. Learn how to manage that fact.

53

BUGGERY

DO NOT GET BUGGERED AT WORK.

Simple stuff.

Do NOT let people take the credit for your work, unless you are in an amazing team and everyone knows the rules (there aren't many of those around yet, unfortunately).

Do NOT let yourself be overlooked and under-valued. Bring your achievements to management attention. Trumpet yourself a bit. A man would.

Get your contract and read it. Make sure you get pay reviews. Check out market rates. Ask for appraisals and go prepared to them.

Do NOT go into business without written agreements. Trust is a myth in business, at least until you've worked together for a time. Document everything and stick it in a drawer in case you ever need it. Unfortunately, the world we live in, whilst mainly being populated by good people, also has some incredibly greedy gits in it. These people are normally fine to work with until there's money to fight over — and then they will stop at literally nothing to get their, and your, share.

In the event that anyone balks at signing legal agreements, run for the hills. It would be like getting married and having him refuse to sign the register. (Jerry, Mick and Bali is all I'm saying.)

All the above assumes that you are a great worker, honest, capable, willing, determined, flexible and valuable. If you're not, expect to be shafted and possibly sacked. That's the deal.

SUTRA: Get it legal then forget about it.

54

THE INVISIBLE WOMAN

Before we end this bit, I wanted to de-bunk a few myths. Talking of de-bunking, can you bunk something? Just a thought.

I've been reading for many years that women become invisible at a certain age. It used to be forty. Then it shifted towards fifty. If you read Jan Moir or Liz Jones in the Daily Mail, all women over fifty should be shut in a cupboard or wear a burqa, so unappealing are they for public viewing.

The worst culprits at levelling criticism at women — often downright cruel criticism — are other women. Newspapers and internet photos of women's aging hands, wrinkly knees, scraggy necks. A horrendous one recently of Angelica Huston, taken at a bad angle, outright slated her for aging badly. This was, and remains, one of the most beautiful, talented and interesting women in world.

She's aged a bit. So have we all, for fuck's sake. Poor Nadine who took my photos for the book and the website has worked like a navvy to make me look good. No photoshopping has been involved but I can tell you that unless the world views me gently back-lit, from an angle of about 40 degrees above the horizontal, and preferably from standing on a chair, I do not look great.

Invisibility at a certain age is utter horseshit.

You don't know me. But I can tell you that I am far from invisible.

In fact, as I age and get more interesting, less concerned with what people think and have more experience and wisdom to bring to the party (and I do like a good party), I find myself more in demand and more visible than ever.

So, do NOT succumb to this ridiculous propaganda.

Look forward to aging. Do so with relish. Look after yourself, keep fit, dress well (or dress however you bloody well want) and allow yourself no limitations or barriers. The best way to get a bikini body? Put on a bikini.

The only way in which I permit you to consider yourself invisible at any time in your life is when you do what you would only do if you thought no one could see you.

Let rip.

SUTRA: You're not invisible. Unless you choose to be.

PINK VIAGRA

I was thinking about what I feel like when I really desire something — or someone... (steady).

Just thinking about it/him, I get a delicious tingle of overwhelming anticipation and excitement — like when you're a child at the top of a helter-skelter and you can't believe the rush of what you're about to experience. Butterflies in my tummy.

Desire invades your mind, draws your thinking and makes you notice things.

You see the back of your lover's head in a crowd. Only it's not him.

You want a red Porsche and see them everywhere.

You long to be pregnant and seem to be surrounded by babies and pregnant women.

Desire is good. It drives us forward. It tells our subconscious the things we want and tells it to look out for them and give us a signal.

And it gives people and the universe the opportunity to give us things that please us.

Desire is only unhelpful when we won't work to get what we want. Lazy desire is just greed by another name.

Desire is having high expectations of and for yourself. It is what creates your reality.

Desire is more than wanting. It's craving, longing, like you do for your lover. It's visceral and it's when you feel most alive.

55

DECISIONS, DECISIONS

I have a friend. She's in her mid sixties and life has become dull, dull, dull. She doesn't know what she wants or what could make a difference, so she doesn't actually do anything. She has forgotten how to desire anything and move Heaven and Earth to get it.

So, faced with things she could do, she can't decide what might work to lift her out of her rut.

She's considered doing some voluntary work. Or writing her family history. Or working in a care home — she used to be a nurse years ago and is good with old people.

She hasn't done any of them yet because she hasn't made her mind up which is best.

Look, in this long, long life you're going to have to make a lot of decisions.

(You do get that you're going to have a long, long life, don't you? Just stop for a moment and consider how old you are now and what has happened up until now. Now roll that forward to you're ninety-five or so. See? Tons of time.)

We worry about decisions. Is it the right one? What if at all goes catastrophically wrong?

The great thing about any decision is that whatever we decide is always the right one. For the simple reason that we will never know the outcome of any alternative decisions.

> *"There is nothing either good or bad, but thinking makes it so."*
>
> *William Shakespeare, Hamlet*

Don't fret. Make choices, do stuff. Change your mind and do other stuff. (Just remember the bit about not quitting too soon or too late. Timing is all.)

Desire things — experiences, success, memories, beauty, travel, love — whatever turns you on.

The biggest thing you can do to 'un-stick' yourself is to realise that *you always have a choice*. If you think you don't have a choice, you're wrong. At the very least you can choose how to think differently about whatever you are facing.

Choose a lot. You don't know if you are choosing wisely or well, but choose. To play, to love, to experiment, to fail, to try, to make mistakes, to come up smelling of roses or land in the shit.

After love, our freedom to choose is the most precious thing of all.

Use it.

SUTRA: Be brave. Just make a decision.

56

RED HOT PASSION

Right, you are visible and you are making choices at a rate of knots. What else?

Be like a kid.

Or a Labrador puppy.

Get into things. Do it with passion and enthusiasm. Do it now and do it fast.

Ignore it if your family or friends say, "Oh, she's off again, on the latest passion/hair-brained scheme." People are quick to criticise anyone who shows real passion because it is a rare and enviable thing. Even when it looks slightly mental.

People have rolled their eyes at my 'passions' all my life. Frequently I have proved them right by abandoning the latest 'next best thing' never to look at it again. So what? It's just another story to tell.

And out of the kaleidoscope of things that I've tried and often abandoned has come the most extraordinary collection of interests and passions that sustain me daily and earn me a living.

Treat your life like steel.

Stick it in fire to temper it, make it strong.

SUTRA: Throw your heart over the bar. Your body will follow.

57

YOUR BEST WORK YET

I've no idea what your best work will be.

But I do know that if you put the effort in, your *Magnus Opus* is there waiting to be found.

I do know that you are living, whatever age you are, in the most exciting times of all.

You have the opportunity to create yourself.

Screw 'finding yourself'. I know of people who choose to do nothing every day and then go off on retreat to 'find themselves'.

Good luck with that.

That's like trying to improve your boxing skills without a punch bag or a sparring partner.

We find our strengths and our talents when we are in ACTION.

Your best work is out there. It absolutely doesn't matter what it is, whether it's one thing or many things.

It's your trail. Create the one you want and leave it behind you as a path for others.

That's your work.

SUTRA: You are living your legacy. Make it great.

IF I SHOW YOU MINE, WILL YOU SHOW ME YOURS?

Sometimes life only makes sense in reverse. You can see what happened that caused changes of direction or missed opportunities.

I have been uniquely blessed to have a life less ordinary — apologies to David and Fran for stealing his words and her tattoo.

I worried about putting this bit in but everyone said it mattered that I could show you that, even if you don't know what you're doing, you can still craft a life out of a fair amount of wreckage. I certainly didn't know what I was doing, apart from surviving and following my in-built need to work, and to be fulfilled and achieve something, anything, with my life.

So, here is the short version. I'll update you in about thirty years. I am not stopping now.

58

LIGHTS, CAMERA, ACTION!

My first ever job was a Saturday job. I was fifteen. And useless.

It was in a camera shop owned by Charles Frank, a lovely old (probably about forty-five at the time but I was fifteen and therefore he HAD to be as old as Moses) Jewish chap.

He paid me £5 for each Saturday. For the first few Saturdays I struggled to accept it as I had done nothing at all but dust shelves and look gormless. I didn't get the buzz I expected to get from 'working'. Mainly because I wasn't.

Over the first few weeks, Mr Frank noticed how often I would end up tinkering with his collection of old scientific instruments by way of making myself look occupied. He had amassed theodolites, tank sights, scales, microscopes — all brass and all of varying vintages and makes. I never did find out what interested him in them except that I suppose cameras fall into that kind of category of technical instrument, so that must have been it.

In the end I spent a year of Saturdays, happily researching and cataloguing Mr Frank's collection. I was good at it. Off to the Mitchell Library with photos and sketches and details (no Google then of course), and slowly, but surely, we built a complete record of everything in the collection. I learned how to research, how to plan work and how to set up a system for recording information.

Plus, if I had been required to, I could have lined up a tank gun on an enemy position faster than loading a film in a box brownie.

It didn't feel like work.

I'd have fired me day one...

59

BLOOD AND BRAINS

Having finished with Mr Frank and his collection, I found myself between 5th and 6th year (old currency) at school. There was no chance of a summer off — work was what we did in our family, not holidays or recreation — so I scouted around for a job.

I had decided to be an engineer. This was for no other reason than that I wanted to please my adoptive father. I was not cut out for it but that seemed no reason not to stubbornly proceed. So I did.

But I couldn't get a job anywhere to do with engineering. To be fair I still didn't know what KIND of engineer I wanted to be. My father was a structural engineer, self taught, and he worked pretty permanently overseas on oil refineries. The only think I knew for sure was that it wouldn't be chemical engineering as chemistry classes made me feel sick.

I eventually got a job as a lab assistant in the Haematology Laboratory of Glasgow Royal Infirmary. I was equally useless there but I felt better about myself because I got to wear a white coat and wander round wards collecting blood samples from nurses.

I was always the one picked to go to the morgue with a plastic basin to collect organs. On one occasion it was a brain. I have no idea why, but it had to be liquefied in what looked like — and actually turned out to be — a Kenwood blender. I expect, in retrospect, that they were simply winding me up. Anyway, I can't eat *crème brûlée* anymore.

For some reason, probably for entertainment purposes, they asked me back the next summer. And I went.

SEWERS AND THIGH HIGH BOOTS

I went to Glasgow University, having settled on Civil Engineering. The decision-making process was not complicated. I didn't like Chemical, I didn't fancy Electrical, and the machines in the Mechanical Engineering building just looked big and boring. That left Civil and Computer — a brand new course that had not taken off and clearly wasn't going anywhere fast. Idiot. I turned it down purely on the basis that I couldn't work out how to make pictures out of holes on the punch cards in the computing lab. The guys could — naked ladies abounded.

I was the only girl in the year.

An engineering degree is unlike most others. I guess it's similar to a medical degree. Five days a week, lectures 9am-1pm and labs 2pm-5pm. It bore no resemblance whatsoever to student life as expected. We also had to do summer work as part of the course.

So, the summer found me working for Glasgow Corporation in the Sewage Department. The sewers, like those of London, were old and leaking. In order to plan maintenance, a record had to be built of the underground map of the sewage system and the flow of 'water' in them. Lucky old me. We put dye down one manhole and waded into the system to see where the dye re-appeared. Thigh-high wellies, a lot of crap and a fair amount of shallow breathing that summer.

Coincidentally, thigh-high boots featured elsewhere that summer and were the start of my portfolio career, if only I had known it. On Gibson Street, near the University, was a shop called Natty Bumppo. The owner made leather clothing. Famously, he made the yellow leather banana for Billy Connolly in his 'Big Yin' days. He used me to model it on.

Anyway, he used to make leather hot pants, trousers and skirts (more like pelmets really) and fashioned thigh-high leather boots by stitching the top onto killer stilettos. He gave me pink suede flares with holes cut all down the sides so they couldn't be worn with knickers. Those were the days. But my size 8 body carried it well, and in exchange for wearing them to discos at University and telling people where I got them from, I got to keep the clothes. I was the funkiest student of them all, for no cash exchanged. One of my earliest 'contra' deals. All I have left is one dodgy photo but oh my, it was fun.

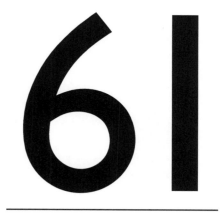

ON THE ROADS

Finally I got let loose on actual engineering. First of all in Glasgow, setting out a block of flats and then with Kesteven County Council, setting out a new road.

And, yes, again I was the only woman. Not just the only woman they had but the only woman they had ever had. When I applied for jobs companies would write back and request a photograph. I'm convinced I only got taken on out of curiosity.

Anyway, being a site engineer was more up my street, so to speak.

It was outside, for a start, in all weathers. It was varied and involved a lot of walking and lugging and lifting. It needed focussed attention to get it right and you had to get on with the team actually laying the road around you.

There were early starts, often in the dark, setting out by the beams of Land Rover headlights, and often late finishes, as we worked to hit deadlines. Allocated my own chain man (a hunk, I recall, but I was too nervous to notice), I didn't have to carry all my own heavy equipment. Bless.

But they were sweet to me, the construction guys, even when I lined up using the wrong side of the long iron 'pin' that you set up with, and made a one inch kink in the kerbing that was visible to the naked eye from 100 yards away. They had to lift it and re-lay. As the men were paid piecework, it meant they lost a day's pay. Not good.

But I learned a few things and not just about engineering. I learned I like responsibility and I like being free. I like taking charge and I can cope with stress, even fear. And I can live with isolation and work on my own as well as with a team.

And I knew that I definitely liked the concept of work, especially when you can see the results of it. And a road — with roundabouts — is a very concrete result of your work. It felt good.

62

GIN AND DENIM

Now, along the way I got married. To a handsome RAF pilot. We got posted to Malta and so I ended up unable to work. As far as I recall, officer's wives weren't allowed (or certainly weren't encouraged) to work in 1975, and certainly there was next to no work to be had in Malta unless you were in the forces.

RAF Luqa had very few married quarters and so we wives were dotted around the island in private rentals.

My husband and I ended up in a little house at the end of a row of Maltese cottages — like a Mediterranean row of terraces — in the north of the island near Salina Bay.

We had no British neighbours — the nearest were at the tip of the bay about a half hour walk away and with the only car needed to get to base for work I was often on foot. We had no television, no telephone and only British Forces Broadcasting on the radio. We got one trip home in our three year posting.

I took myself off to a Pitman Script course in Valletta. I have no idea why, I guess I just needed something to do. The rest of the time was, to be fair, fun. We had a speedboat, a lot of very cheap gin, and good friends. It was probably the last knockings of the good old days for the military abroad. But it was crucifying if you wanted to work or keep yourself occupied. But obviously having a baby (David) was a good diversion.

Malta taught me to be self-sufficient. Weeks at a time with no husband, a baby to look after, no relatives to help and little diversion make for a pretty resilient person.

In the latter months we met a Maltese businessman who for some reason thought I had a good head on my shoulders. He was manufacturing denim jeans and persuaded me that I should import them to Scotland when we were posted back. My husband, bless him, supported me in this mad venture.

Back in Forres, we became the importers and ultimately the owners of the finest collection of denim flares in the north. I think we sold about ten pairs in total.

And I learned my first (harsh) lesson in business.

63

ALL IN MY HEAD

Once back in Scotland, baby number two, Frances, arrived. This time life was easier. Our families lived in Glasgow and so could travel up to see us more, and although my husband was away a lot, everything was manageable.

I got time to read and to contemplate what to do next.

But, *but*. I was not cut out for full time Officer's Wife stuff. My husband had been promoted and was now a Squadron Leader and captain of a crew, but I simply didn't feel at ease with coffee mornings and my flower arranging skills were entirely missing. (They still are. That's what florists are for.)

I was a big reader. Books have always been important to me and when the kids were little I was a benignly neglectful mother, letting them amuse themselves whilst I read. I also was becoming restless. My brain needed to do something but I didn't know what. Going back to engineering was out of the question with two small babies and a husband frequently on detachment.

Around this time, I came across a copy of *The Tao of Physics* by Fritrof Capra. It blew my mind.

This was a book talking about the common ground between Eastern mysticism and Western physics. It talked about consciousness as a 'thing'. I was hooked.

GETTING PHYSICAL

It seemed to me that if I didn't work out how to work I would ultimately go mad. The kids were coming up to three and five and soon they would be at nursery and school. What the hell do you do with your days once that happens?

It was impossible to find a job and I had no idea what to do.

Spurred on by the *Tao of Physics*, I researched how I could train as a teacher. My husband was supportive. Fortunately, although he couldn't control his time — when a Nimrod has to go on Search and Rescue, it has to go — he was a very hands-on dad and could perfectly competently run the house. So, between him and the helpful mothers of local kids, we cobbled together a plan.

Which, on reflection, was mental.

Aberdeen College was two hours (80 miles) away by car. But car was not the way to do it as the roads were narrow and windy, traffic heavy and snow almost certain (this is taking place mainly over the winter in the North of Scotland). I used to get up at 5.30 am, get the ice off my Mini Cooper, drive to Forres station, park, get on a train to Aberdeen (not a guaranteed event by any stretch, especially if a cow had wandered onto the line), get on a bus in Aberdeen and then walk to college for lectures at 9am.

Then reverse the exercise at night, getting home about 8.30pm.

Fortunately, it was only for one academic year and two months were spent doing a teaching practice locally. We all survived. Just.

That qualified me as a teacher of Maths and Physics, which I then cheerfully did at Lossiemouth, and then as Head of Physics at a school in Oxford when we were posted South.

Thus, I proved to myself that I loved teaching. Unfortunately, I then discovered that I hated teachers more.

65

MAMMON

Now living in Buckinghamshire, I had settled into a Head of Department job in Oxford. Whilst still teaching — Oxbridge entrance Physics now — I got involved in the business of the college. It was not a cheery experience. I was surrounded by glitteringly clever people with no common sense and a rigid set of rules.

It was stultifying and I wanted out.

I had continued my reading and research on consciousness and the workings of our brains and minds. I was hugely interested in the mind/body connection, how we learned, what makes us who we are, and how to be the best we can be. I was, to be fair, open to everything.

I assumed that as a bright and capable thirty-five year old, I would have no problem finding work. As Head of Department I had to give two terms notice, a full six months. Surely that was plenty of time to find a new job?

Nope.

I fell into financial services. This was 1986. The City and the whole business of financial services was cowboy territory. I hated it with a passion. Products were being sold by people with no morals to people with no knowledge. Investments that made no sense were being concocted and the companies that flogged them couldn't care less. No Google, no Internet, no way to compare or learn. It was, as we were all to discover some time later, a house of cards.

So, what do you do when you get into a new industry about which you know very little, which seems to be corrupt and about which it is very hard to learn if you come at it late in life?

You start your own business and decide to change the world of course.

And, six years later, by 1992, I had grown a very nice little business.

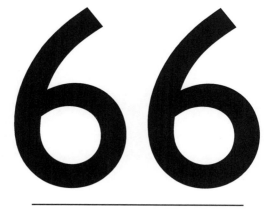

COITUS INTERRUPTUS

In 1988 I had got divorced. It was horrendous. In my life and business I battled on in a tough climate of high interest rates and rising inflation.

Finally my body gave up. In 1993, I couldn't last any longer. I had been falling asleep at the wheel of my car, collapsing, being sick, unable to sleep at night but unable to stay awake in the day, aching constantly, too tired to walk or climb stairs, even to brush my hair. My brain had stopped working and I thought I was going mad.

I was finally and mercifully diagnosed with ME — chronic fatigue syndrome — or as it was known then, yuppie flu.

I lost pretty much everything. I was told I would never work again and handed my business over to the new junior partner I had taken on. With a brain like mush, I kept no shares. I ended up on state benefits.

I spent seven years getting better and when I finally did I was a different person. Not totally rebuilt but a long way towards knowing what rebuilt would look like.

I knew one thing for sure. What goes on inside your head decides what goes on in your world.

I got back into my old business but this time as an employee not an owner. Over time I earned a small amount of stock options and when it was sold I got some cash — not much, but every little helps. Unless something dramatic happens, I shall have to work forever. I don't mind. Not now.

Because what I really learned when I was sick and in the six years I was back in my old business, first as Operations Director and finally as CEO, was to work out what I could and couldn't do, what I was good at and what I wasn't, what I liked and what I didn't.

Most importantly, I finally worked out what I was prepared to put up with and what I wasn't.

67

OLDER AND WISER

Whilst recovering from ME and back at my old company, I decided to learn a few more things. I already knew I would probably have to work forever, and it had dawned on me that I was still not as happy as I could be in myself, and that I was definitively not 'in flow' at work. As I looked around me I saw the same in other people. Too much stress, too little focus on what really matters. All of us focussed on today's problems and disconnected from what we did to cause them in the first place.

And fear. A lot of fear. Fear of failure, of success (yes really), of making money, losing money, being the right person, never becoming the right person, being beaten by someone, of being passed by, losing a business, building a business, of speaking up, not speaking up, of loneliness, of being with the wrong person — God, the list was endless.

So I studied. I took courses. Dear God, I took courses. My kids thought I was mental and possibly I was. I bought books. No, I devoured books, CDs, seminars and more than once I thought I had stumbled on the Holy Grail. I hadn't. I had more likely stumbled over the piles of books and CDs and credit card receipts as I searched for what? Me? Fuck knows.

But here is what I accumulated. I accumulated knowledge and skills. All by accident, of course. Sort of a 'throw enough mud at the wall and it will stick' type of thing. Not structured at all. No Zen was involved in this transformation, but a shed load of curiosity and energy was.

And I started working with other people and their businesses. I took over a head-hunting firm and was CEO for three years. I worked with all sorts of businesses. Sports, IT, spas, golf courses, retail, digital media. I coached people. I set up a mentoring group for smaller businesses. I lubricated the fuck out of everyone I knew, adding value, making connections, helping out.

I became a Master NLP practitioner (vastly over-populated now I'm afraid but still useful if you take it with a pinch of salt), a 'thought field therapist' (weird but amazing and it works), a hypnotherapist (don't stand near me if you don't want to buy me a drink).

I got a voice and I started using it.

And I discovered that business is business is business and I am damn good at helping businesses and the people who run them.

I discovered what I am for.

68

COMING TOGETHER

So, where am I now?

Well, I reckoned it would only be worth writing this book if I had pulled off its message myself. I really wanted anyone reading it to believe in the possibility of creating their own life, if they want that.

This is what I do and where my life is now:

- I live in London in an apartment I love. One of my lifetime aims was to live in the capital and I still walk home through Kensington Palace Gardens and think how incredibly lucky I am.

- I have friends and neighbours who enhance my life more than I can say.

- I am healthier than I have ever been, due to that personal trainer. I ride to the gym, summer and winter, at 6.30am two mornings a week and at 9.30am on Saturday. I am a fit and healthy. I am never sick.

- I am more comfortable in my skin than I have ever been. I am over sixty but feel about forty and have as much fun as I did then — possibly more.

- I work with a number of clients — oil trading, IVF, sports, brand management, Internet, wealth management, technology — I am constantly upgrading clients as I see fit and I am regularly approached to take on new clients.

- I am slowly taking on more non-executive director roles so that I can skew my work towards speaking and writing, whilst maintaining my income. I have also carved out more time to spend with my family and friends.

- I use and teach my hippy trippy stuff like NLP and TFT as and when. It's become blended into my life. (See, it wasn't all bollocks.)

- I write for *Management Today* magazine as 'Madame Guillotine'.

- I plan another book shortly.

- I have more plans and projects than I know what to do with. It's hugely exciting.

- I meet fascinating, successful and often sexy people.

- My sex life? Mind your own business!

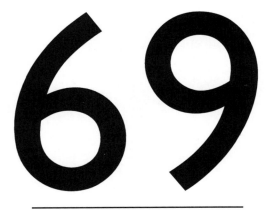

69

HAPPY ENDINGS

One thing I like a lot about life is that we never know what's in store for us. We don't have to worry about the bad stuff because most of it will never happen and if it does, we'll cope because that's what we do. So, there's no need to spend even a moment fretting about what bad things might happen.

And when the lovely surprises turn up, it's like being a child again. Delight in discovering a new talent, a new passion, a new love. Delight in being sixty-one and more in love with life than ever.

And some of the bad times — there's no denying they happened is there? But of course, now it's not the bad shit. It's the stuff that made me. That makes me.

Your bad shit will make you. If you can grasp that early enough on, you might start to welcome challenges and adversity for what they give you in the long run.

We are living in wonderfully uncertain times. There are more opportunities than you imagine.

You can, you MUST, design the life you want.

Even if you can only feel the breeze of change now, it will become a hurricane. Tether yourself to something solid — you, your talents, your passions and your pleasure.

You can and will find that the world has so arranged itself — and will do so even more — to make a long life of fulfilling work more than possible. In the middle of it, your work in all its forms will hold you through all the travelling you will do — emotionally, practically, financially and geographically.

And at the end, you will truly become the person you came here to be.

Apply what is in here. Pay attention, and watch how you have more power than you ever thought possible.

And at the core of all you do, remember that you can get everything you want by giving other people what they need.

And it's no coincidence that this last chapter is number 69.

THANKS

There are loads of people to thank. Everyone who ever took a chance and employed me. Everyone I work with now — they enthuse and inspire me daily. Everyone who has ever allowed me to teach them something, because that's the greatest privilege of all.

Patsy Heavey — aka Patsy Pitstop — is my dear friend and neighbour. She has read, commented, critiqued and scribbled on every page of the numerous incarnations of this book. Patsy, thanks for all that and putting up with my obsession for writing this but especially for allowing me to have a generous, champagne drinking, hilarious friend who happens to be called Patsy. I couldn't make you up.

To everyone who read the early drafts and came back with brutal honesty, thanks. I've stopped crying now.

To Esther Harris, my editor — thanks for the support and the kickings and thank fuck we've finally finished. Sorry this has been more painful than giving birth (and with a considerably longer gestation period).

To my dear friend Nadav Kander for suggesting Mark Tappin and Simon Gofton who made the beautiful cover for the book. Legends, all.

To Nadine Burzler for somehow conjuring up decent pictures of me without resorting to anything more than a shed-load of talent, about 350 shots and biblical patience. And also for the wonderful website she designed and set up. Generosity beyond compare.

To Amy Harris for pitching in out of nowhere and for nothing to work with Nadine to get this out into the world. Marketing ninjas, both of them.

Lastly to my little family — David, Fran, Nicole, Archie and Harvey. I have no words for how much I love you.

ABOUT THE AUTHOR

Avril Millar has been, and is, many things — an engineer, teacher, wealth manager, businesswoman, mentor, writer, speaker, turnaround expert, non-executive director and chairwoman. She has lived, and continues to live, the life and work she writes about here. With five different careers under her belt already, she anticipates a few more before they nail the lid down. She is the mother of a grown-up son and daughter, a besotted grandmother of two and the proud owner of a bus pass. And she still doesn't know what to do if she ever grows up. But she's excited about the possibilities...

PRINTED AND BOUND BY:

Copytech (UK) Limited trading as Printondemand-worldwide,
9 Culley Court, Bakewell Road, Orton Southgate. Peterborough,
PE2 6XD, United Kingdom.